The People

South Shields

by

John Carlson & Joyce Carlson

Tyne Dock, 1951. Father Leo B. Landreth and children of the Parish of St Peter and Paul's Roman Catholic Church in Belle Vue Crescent. The occasion is the visit of HMS *Superb* to the Dock.

Previous Page
Making hay at Cleadon Laws Farm around 1935. The view is towards the general direction of Cleadon Water Tower. The farm house was demolished in 1965 and the site is now occupied by Carnoustie Drive. On the right is the late Harry Wray, father of Robert Wray and the nephew of the owners of the farm Ralph and Edith Colley. On the left is his Royal Air Force colleague Tim.

Copyright © John Carlson & Joyce Carlson 1998

First published in 1998 by

The People's History
Suite 1
Byron House
Seaham Grange Business Park
Seaham
Co. Durham
SR7 0PW

ISBN 1 902527 20 8

Contents

South Shields Corporation bus No 104 stands at Tyne Dock. If the bus is ahead of time the driver will be having a few minutes break before the run up to Simonside.

Introduction

This book is not a history of South Shields, but an anthology of information, photographs and moments of personal history.

Most of the personal recollections are from interviews that took place in 1998. Others have been transcribed from a variety of diaries and documents, some dating back prior to 1850, the year Queen Victoria granted the town the status of a borough. While in all cases the compilers have attempted to retain both the contributors' words and meaning, some editing has been undertaken to ease the flow of the text.

The recollections of Town Clerk, Robert Salmon, are taken from records of a lecture he gave in 1856 Newspaper extracts are from the *Shields Gazette* unless otherwise stated.

A number of books have proved useful in preparation of the text, including the *Tramways of Jarrow and South shields* by George S. Herse, *The Harton Electric Railway* by Bill Hatcher, *From Tazziz to Tyneside* by Richard I. Lawless.

CHICHESTER CORNER SOUTH SHIELDS (463)

Chichester Corner, *circa* 1910. Next to the junction of King Street and Fowler Street, this was probably the town's most important crossroads. Almost all of the buildings remain today, yet almost everything is different.

Members of the Glebe Church on stage in their 1930 production of *The Minister's Wife's New Bonnet*.

Acknowledgements

Many people have helped in the production of this book. I would particularly like to thank Geordie Atkinson, Marrian Allen, Alf Beris, Dennis Boad, Olga Carlson, Ken Carter, Jean Cockayne, Barry Dobson, Elizabeth Edmund, Marion Fay, Norman Fay, Malcolm Grady, Ken Goodall, Beatrice Green, Muriel Hanson, Alan Havery, Beryl Henderson, Terry Henderson, Bill Henderson, Jean Henderson, Bob Jewitt, Lorna Johnston, Harry Lowe, Abdo Mohamed Kaid, Evelyn Lawson, Bill Lodge, Robert Mack, Arthur Meeks, Joan Meeks, Cuthbert Nicholson, Kathleen Nicholson, Arthur Pegler, Eric Pollard, Eddie Post, George Post, Bill Reeve, Dorothea Shell, Matty Smith, Sarah Smith, Stuart Smith, Robert Wray, Emma Wilson and Irene Wilson.

I am also grateful for the help of Keith Bardwell and Doris Johnson of South Tyneside Libraries, who would welcome seeing those old photos before you chuck them out, Newcastle City Libraries, the Tyne and Wear Archive Service, Beamish The North Of England Open Air Museum Archive and Tramway staff and the staff of the *Shields Gazette*. I would also like to thank James Cleet, Amy Flagg, Robert F. Mack and all of those past photographers and writers, both famous and forgotten, without whom the recorded history of the town would be much sparser.

Finally I would also like to thank Dave Dean, Daniel Lushman, Andrew Clark, Craig Wainright and everyone at The Tanfield Railway, Oxfam Books, Newcastle University Politics Department and Library Staff, CRU, The League of Friends Library and all the staff and patients of Ward 2 at South Shields General Hospital over April/May 1998.

THE MARKET AND TEMPLETOWN

The Market ... The Old Town Hall ... St Hilda Pit ... The Gas Works ... The Mill Dam ...

Town Hall and Market Place. South Shields

A general view of the Market Square, *circa* 1900. Prominent buildings are the Town Hall, St Hilda's Church and St Hilda Pit. To the right of the old Town Hall is the Tramcar Hotel. An account of a visit to the area in 1886 stated that: 'To the stranger who arrives at the South Shields Station, the first view of the town is anything but promising. Right opposite is that classic place called the Cinder Hill which appears to have been the scene of some convulsion of nature from the uneven surface and remains of pottery that are strewn about. To the right are the picturesque rubbish hills of St Hilda Pit. To the left is that gloomy structure St Hilda's Church which is always in mourning, having a clock which for sheer bashfulness always keeps its hands before its unwashed face.'

A Town Falls Into Place

In 1900 the New Town Hall would be in the planning stages; horse tram tracks would run from the Pier Head, through King Street, around the far side of the market, then through Templetown to Tyne Dock where, each year, around six million tons of coal and coke would trundle across the arches and into the holds of waiting colliers. This, reportedly, was the largest amount from any single dock in the world at that time. The population of the town would be slightly greater than 100,000.

The Old Town Hall would be just over one hundred and thirty years old in 1900. Domestic gas lighting would have been in place since 1823. St Hilda Pit had opened in 1825 and steam locomotives arrived in the town in 1834. 1850 was quite a year with an experimental electric lighting system installed on the Lawe Top, The Tyne Improvement Commission meeting for the first time and Queen Victoria granting the town its charter of incorporation making it the borough of South Shields. Around that time Methodist John Wesley reportedly preached in the Market Square. The Cleadon Well was sunk in 1864, and began extracting over a quarter of a million gallons of water a day. The Alhambra Music Hall which seated over three thousand people, opened its doors in 1873. The Corporation's electric power station in Holburn began generating electricity in August 1896. The flags came out for Queen Victoria's Diamond Jubilee in 1897. William Robson QC would win South Shields for the Liberals in the 1900 general election, their seventeenth successive victory since 1832. A public subscription would be launched in 1901 to fund the statue of Queen Victoria that now stands outside the Town Hall. Clean running electric trams would appear on the streets of Shields in 1906 and along with the internal combustion engine and the airship they would be seen as the heralds of a new century of science, prosperity and peace.

Left: An illustration for the official programme of Chapter Row Wesleyan Centenary Bazaar of 1909. The central illustration depicts the Market Place around 1850. From its construction in 1768 by the Dean and Chapter of Durham, until 1910 when the town council moved out to the present town hall in Beach Road, most of the town's affairs were run from the Old Town Hall. The Dean and Chapter had owned the market and largely run the town until Queen Victoria granted South Shields a Charter of Incorporation in 1850, the town became a borough and an elected town council took over. The 1853 South Shields Improvement Act allowed the Corporation to buy the building, the market and associated tolls for £500, which they did in 1855.

Incorporation came about largely through public dissatisfaction with the development of the town. Trade on the Tyne had long been dominated by the City of Newcastle and there was a widespread feeling that South and North Shields needed their own voice. A contemporary prospectus for the *North and South Shields Gazette* reads:

'It is believed … that there does not exist anywhere else in Great Britain at the present day, so large and compact a trading community as that of Shields so deplorably ill represented by the trading press. Dependent on the rival towns of Newcastle and Sunderland for the means of appearing before the public, the influence of Shields has been largely swamped, while here interests, habitually forgotten, have, wherever a jealous rivalry exists, been seriously (may we not say systematically) damaged or even sometimes betrayed.

In making these allusions, there is no intention to tear open old sores … such things only show how essential to our welfare must be the possession of the means, which a vigorous local print will afford, of stating our views, vindicating our own cause when assailed, and of rebutting where necessary, the united and powerful efforts of a press which has proved but too unanimous in its enmity to those infant energies of Shields.'

Additionally, census information was revealing how poor conditions were for the majority of people. Documentation suggests that the town's fresh water supply was badly polluted and discounting drinking water could only provide a pint per person each day for every other use. Sanitation was almost non-existent and even the middle classes suffered badly in the 1832 and 1848 Cholera epidemics. Policing was also minimal.

Town Clerk, Robert Salmon wrote: 'The streets as well as carriageways and footways, were badly paved, insufficiently cleansed and totally unlighted. Houses were built according to the interested motives of those who obtained sites from the Dean and Chapter of Durham. No regulating or restraining authority existed on the part of the public. Numerous swine of the most disgusting description wallowed unmolested in the unwholesome sump holes of the public thoroughfare – foul water and filthy offal were cast with impunity upon our streets – the public and private middens were full even to overflowing – and in the absence of scavenger carts for the daily reception of the ashes, dirt and refuse of the inhabitants, the state of the houses middens and conveniences may really be conceived.'

The east side of the Market Square, *circa* 1900. Crofton's Department Store stands to the left. They appear to be having a sale. After the building was destroyed in the Second World War, the site was used as a static water tank for the auxiliary fire service. The Tram Hotel is visible on the right.

Grey wet cobblestones and roofs in the late 1930s. A lone Whelks stall stands ready for business. Businessman Arthur Pegler recalls: 'The butchers stalls used to be at the ferry side of the market. When the ferry's boilers were stoked up black smoke would trail across the market, so heaven only knows what condition the meat was in. There was a small man with a loud voice who had a stall beside St Hilda's Church. There was always a crowd around the stall. He would put eight half crowns along the front of the stall, blow up a paper bag with his mouth, pop in an apple, an orange and a pear and then he would pick up a half crown, try it in his teeth to show the crowd it was real, then bang it in the bag and shout, 'A Tanner!' There was always a rush to buy these bags. I watched that man week after week and eventually I bought a bag for sixpence. I went around the back of St Hilda's Church, stuffed the fruit in my pockets, felt in the bottom of the bag and, no half crown! I was nearly in tears on my way home.'

An advertisement for Crofton's Department Store, 1909.

Market Day, *circa* 1962. Jack Reeve is sitting on the scales while his brothers George and Jimmy look on. The large building at the back right is Woolworth's; the site of Crofton's Department Store remained undeveloped until the mid 1960s.

The interior of the offices of J. Barbour and Son Ltd waterproof clothing manufacturers, situated on the west side of the Market Square.

Corporation trolleybuses in the Market Square, *circa* 1960. The conductors are removing the trolley poles from the overhead wire to allow the bus at the back, the No 4 for Tyne Dock, to go through. Bus Inspector Barry Dobson recalls: 'Most of the corporations stored the trolley retriever pole under the bus so if another pulled up behind you, you couldn't get it out. South Shields Corporation were almost unique in that theirs was stored on the side. The market cafe next to Norman Richardson's Newsagents had a contract to supply us with hot water for our tea for only a penny. It was two pence everywhere else.'

Motorbus No 102 pulls out for Marsden. Ex-conductor Dennis Boad recalls: 'In 1951 I was courting my wife to be, Beryl, who worked at the Odeon Billiard Saloon. At the market I would tell the driver, 'I'll be away for about five minutes,' and would run to see her. Once, I was away a few minutes more than I should. The driver just saw the platform was clear in the mirror and left. He was turning up Fowler Street with me running a long way behind before one of the passengers told him, 'You've got no conductor!' The evening buses from the Market were crammed with shipyard workers. We could hardly get through the gangways to collect the fares. You had to be 'forceful' – you were the captain of the ship and if passengers became rowdy you had to handle it and there was a bell code for the driver to stop the bus and help you out. When that didn't work we would just drive the bus to the police station.'

A trolleybus runs down Station Road to the roundabout on the junction with Commercial Road, 1963. The La Strada Club is on the right. Around this time gambling was allowed on the premises and the club would be attracting top name acts. The club's Continental nature chimed with the times as most people were then having foreign holidays for the first time.

A membership card or 'passport' for the La Strada Club.

The construction of Kepple Street to the south and developments to the north have shorn King Street of much of is surrounding buildings and clutter. Although the names of Union Alley, East Street and Chapter Row still appear on streetmaps, their character is now very different to this late 1940s depiction of the district:

'Three Arabs walked in front of me from East Holburn to the Market Place. They stopped there to be decorated with fourpenny sprigs of Mistletoe which sprayed across their coat lapels. They then walked into the street of light and life – into King Street. It is a street brilliant with signs that flash in and out: arcs and windows of light. An invitation to theatres and cinemas. That is King Street at night. And there is the street behind.

An automatic piano agitated by the prodigal patronage of a penny in a slot was hammering itself completely out of tune with its surroundings. Three foreign seafarers whom I took to be Scandinavians, sat near the mechanical musician. Many more people came into the brightly lighted room; the greater numbers of the visitors women. Women of various ages; possibly of various purposes. Two girls, pretty still in spite of the powders and rouge and carmine that illuminated their faces. Others in the room were in the twenties; some in the thirties – and harsh and course of tongue and feature. They smoked cigarettes and drank stout and beer.

This of course was perfectly permissible; even reasonable. A notice in the inn plainly stated that a reasonable time is allowed to ladies for refreshment. I stayed an almost unreasonable time; and some who had come in early were there when I went out. Men came in, and went away. Some of the women went out; some came back again. Some did not come back. Others did not go out. The three Arabs gorgeously came into the room. The overwhelming glory of their raiment had not been apparent until they strode into the lighted room. Trilby hat with the crown full out, white collar, black and white bow tie, bright red undervest, with a white slip showing behind it and a short tweed waistcoat over it, tweed coat and trousers, brown kid gloves, spats and red boots. That was all on one. Joseph would have turned his coat into lost luggage had there been competition such as this in Egypt. The night grew old. I made other calls. In one brightly lit buffet were two well dressed girls in furs. The girl smoked cigarettes in an expensive manner throwing them to the fire after a few puffs of each.

I looked into other places where the lights still glowed. In one, four young men in their early twenties were keenly playing dominoes though otherwise they appeared to be quite intelligent. In another inn two apprentice seamen, gold braided, stout sombrely drinking alone. They went out at the stroke of ten and moved in the direction of the Market Square into which the lighted buildings were pouring men of all nationalities. The movement is always to the light and brightness of the town.'

The Tyne Dock Engineering Co. Ltd, *circa* 1960. Known locally as 'The Market Dock'. In the foreground, steel plate in the stockyard is being lifted by the yard's vintage mobile crane. In the cab is the late Harry Wray. The crane is about to transport the plate into the yard, with the lifting gang accompanying it to keep it balanced on the chain hoist. Thrift Street runs across the centre ground.

The Chipchase patent liferaft being tested on the Tyne near the TDE yards during the Second World War. On board are several workmen from the yard. The craft could be very quickly launched from a ship that had sustained major damage.

Smiles and waves from the 1st South Shields Sea Scout Troop of the Congregational Church in Ocean Road. Senior scouts and family members are departing from the Market Ferry Landing for North Shields Commissioners Quay, August 1952. They were en route to the seaport town of Haugesund in Norway on the mailboat *Jupiter* for a holiday as guests of the 5th Haugesund Scout Troop.

They stayed with Norwegian families for two weeks enjoying a civic welcome and a reception in the Town Hall with a few days combined camp at Vargeness. Included are; John and George Allen, Alan Byers, Ken Gibson, Robert Wray, Ronnie Tinmouth, Billy Robertshaw, George Overton, Jackie Coates, Jimmy Bruce, Victor Cross, Assistant Scoutmaster Ronnie Drew and his wife Evelyn, children Alan and Margaret and Scoutmaster George Smith.

Another group of people ready to depart on another kind of voyage. The location is just a few yards away from the Ferry Landing, the Ferry Tavern is in the background. NCB Electric Locomotive No E10 is pulling an inspection coach, designed to haul visiting dignitaries around and between the pits of Harton, Westoe, Whitburn and Boldon. Here it is being used to transport enthusiasts around the electric system. Today it

performs a similar function at the Bowes Railway in Gateshead while E10 is preserved a few miles away at the Tanfield Railway.

A London and North Eastern Railway electrical multiple unit, No 23249, wrecked in the sidings below River Drive during an air raid in 1941. The electric service was introduced to Shields in 1938, although most of the stock had been originally built by the North Eastern Railway for use on North Tyneside. The sidings were built in 1834 by the Stanhope and Tyne Railway and originally fanned out above what later became Brigham & Cowan's to feed the company's riverside coal drops. Probably the first steam locomotive in South Shields was placed on the tracks near here in 1834. Although the S&T planned a dock holding around sixteen colliers, financial problems scuppered much of the project and the NER finally sold most of the land to Brigham's in 1905. One of the arches survived in the yard until the site was cleared in the early 1980s.

A rundown looking Thrift Street in 1932. Almost centre are the offices of the Lawson-Batey Tugboat Company with a company tug visible behind. To the left stands Mrs J. Oliver's fruit shop. Lawson-Batey remained in Thrift Street until their offices were damaged by a German bomb landing in the TDE dry-dock in 1941. They then located to the offices of John Cowie and Co. Ltd in Ferry Street.

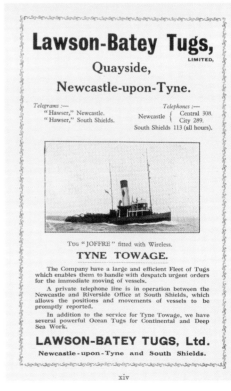

Lawson-Batey Tugs,
LIMITED,

Quayside,
Newcastle-upon-Tyne.

Telegrams :—
" Hawser," Newcastle.
" Hawser," South Shields.

Telephones :—
Newcastle { Central 308.
City 289.
South Shields 113 (all hours).

Tug "JOFFRE" fitted with Wireless.

TYNE TOWAGE.

The Company have a large and efficient Fleet of Tugs which enables them to handle with despatch urgent orders for the immediate moving of vessels.

A private telephone line is in operation between the Newcastle and Riverside Office at South Shields, which allows the positions and movements of vessels to be promptly reported.

In addition to the service for Tyne Towage, we have several powerful Ocean Tugs for Continental and Deep Sea Work.

LAWSON-BATEY TUGS, Ltd.
Newcastle-upon-Tyne and South Shields.

xiv

A 1930 Lawson-Batey advertisement.

The construction of Brigham & Cowan Dry Dock in October 1956. Thomas E. Brigham and Malcolm C. Cowan started out in the engineering trade in 1874 from premises in Corstorphine Town. They later moved to Middle Dock, became a limited liability company in 1900 and moved to Whapping Street in 1905. Building this yard involved the demolition of a row of shops and houses and the rebuilding of two pubs. The yard absorbed the docks of Hepple and Co. in 1924 and Whapping Street itself after the opening of River Drive from Comical Corner to Long Row in 1934.

Mr Brigham opens the 1967 Bowling Season at the North Marine Park. Among those present are; Derrick Pattinson, Billy Charlton (sec), Keith Edmed, Ronnie Scales, Perry Pattinson, Harry Fleck, Alec Downs and Bill Coe (doorman).

An inspection party standing in the yard of St Hilda Colliery around 1902. The engine house is on the left. One of the squat steam locomotives employed to drag wagons under Station Road to the staithes behind the market can be seen. The town gasworks would be to the right. Coal production in Shields began at Templetown Pit on Easter Monday, 1810. Led by the band of the East Yorkshire Militia, miners and their families walked with the coal wagons to the Tyne where the coal was loaded on to Temple's vessel, *The Maida*, named after a victory over the French in Spain. Temple celebrated with a great dinner in Hylton Castle and gave a wagon of coal to local families who had men held captive by the French. In 1820, financial problems forced Temple to sell up to John and Robert Brandling. In 1825 they sank St Hilda.

In 1839 a gas explosion ripped through the St Hilda workings killing 51 men and boys. Local wine merchant James Mather was in one of the first rescue parties inside. He wrote:

We encountered in one place five bodies who had died from the effects of the gas and apparently died quite placidly without one muscle of the face distorted. Then there were three more that had been destroyed by the explosion. Clothes burnt and torn-hair singed off the skin and flesh torn away in several places with an expression as if the spirit had passed away in great agony. We encountered two men, one with a light, the other bearing something on his shoulders; it was a blackened mass – a poor dead burnt boy he was taking out. A little further away we found wagons that had been loaded with coal overturned bottom upwards, a horse laying dead with his head turned over on his shoulder as if in falling he had made a last effort to escape. One man was brought to the surface in a fainting state; he was questioned as to how he felt. 'I am not well sir' he said. 'I have two sons in there.'

Another inspection party at St Hilda Pithead. An 1886 account of a journey down the shaft by a similar party notes that: 'As we descended the air became hotter and more difficult to breathe but after a minute or two we found ourselves in a profound darkness and a cooler atmosphere. In a short time came a glare of light, an appearance of a cavernous sort of place with black dirty walls about, rows of coal tubs, a warm earthy smell mingled with the odour of stables and we found ourselves at the bottom. We followed our guide along a passage about six or seven feet in breadth and the same in height when we came to a great roaring furnace – this was the ventilator. It rarefies the air and an atmospheric stream sets towards it from all parts of the mine and while we were descending the fireman had put on more coals so we got the full benefit of the smoke. Down the main passage or rolleyway we now followed our guide who stopping at a little wooden cabin, invited us in and presented to each of us a woollen jacket with immense pockets, which we put on over our coats, and lighting two Davy lamps we proceeded along till we came to the stables. The horses appeared to be in capital condition, numbering between 40 and 50, some of them rejoicing in names such as Jupiter and Smiley, the warm air making their coats sleek. Our guide having chosen a very quiet animal, yoked him to a rolley with two planks laid on the top on which we had to sit closely packed together. With a gee-up off we went up the uneven rolleyway along dreary passages the roof supported by innumerable props, the rolley jumping and pitching like a ship in a storm. On our way we passed numerous openings, which no doubt led to unutterable darkness. After a half hour's ride we reached a point near the workings and getting off our conveyance we crept into a low and roughly cut tunnel about three feet each way. After passing through a trap door we found ourselves in what is called a chamber or board, the floor heaped with loose coal the roof supported by short props, and picks and shovels lying in all directions; and I must confess it was with a strange feeling I looked around and saw in the walls of coal the remains of the dense forests which covered the Earth during the carboniferous period. We were now about two and a half miles from the shaft and not far from the Lizard Lane. Just above Marsden Rock there is a communication with Harton Pit which is facetiously called by the miners, Harton Back Lane. By means of this communication a strong current of air is continuously passing from Harton to Hilda. Groping our way back to our rolley we seated ourselves and off we went at a sharp trot. Stopping at the mouth of a dark passage to our left, our guide informed us that this was the place where 51 poor fellows lost their lives in the explosion of 1838. Here one of our company showed a strong inclination to faint, but telling him to keep his heart up, we mounted again and soon reached the stables from which we walked in a single file to the bottom of the shaft which is 140 fathoms in depth. Harton being six and a quarter fathoms deeper. We got into the cage, and with a lingering look behind, were hoisted to the top in safety very much pleased with our morning's ramble.'

Right: An electric coal cutter supplied to the Harton Coal Company around 1900 by Messrs W.T. Goolden & Co. of London.

Left: An enamelled Harton Coal Company merchants sign.

Groups of men sitting around 'on their honkers' were a common sight in the 1920s and '30s. Here the reason is a miners' day strike. The location is Claypath Lane with St Hilda Colliery behind it. Now this area is largely covered by a DIY store.

Coal being sorted and graded on the picking belts at St Hilda.

The interior of the winding house at St Hilda, *circa* 1900. In 1908 the steam engines which drove the winder were replaced with 6,000 volt electric motors.

A NCB crew working on the overhead wiring at St Hilda Sidings. Bill Henderson is on the right. A waggonway was opened up along this site in 1832 to transport waste ballast from ships docking at Cookson's Plate Glass Co. at the Mill Dam via Erskine Road to the Bents where it was dumped into ballast hills. After water replaced sand as ballast around 1850, sand began to be hauled back to the Mill Dam for use in glassmaking. In 1882, the Harton Coal Company bought and cleared the glassworks site and built what became known as Harton Staithes. The waggonway was rebuilt to connect with the Marsden Rattler at the Bents allowing coal trains from Boldon and Harton to reach Shields via what is now Chichester Metro Station. In 1989 the railway was replaced by a conveyor belt. With the closure of Westoe in 1993 most of the route has become cycleway.

Two views of the town taken in the 1960s by Bill Henderson from the top of the lighting towers at the St Hilda Yard.

The Patent Fuel works at St Hilda. The old South Shields to Newcastle railway is in the front. Looming in the background is the gas holder. The South Shields Gas company was formed on 17th March 1824. Capital was £4,000 raised by the issue of 160 £25 shares. Gas began to be supplied to shops and houses in October 1824 and to thirty-eight public lamps in November 1829. By 1856 there were 2,000 customers.

Robert Salmon wrote: 'To those of my fellow townsmen who had to perambulate our dark and narrow streets at night, when lanterns were, but cabs were not, in common use and servant maids were in all quarters to be met, bearing their gaily painted green and red lanterns in solemn state before their equally solemn mistresses, the safety and comfort derived from lighting the streets with gas may readily be imagined.'

In 1938 the Company was amalgamated with the Newcastle and Gateshead Gas Company. On the night of 25th August 1940 fifteen bombs fell on the site. During the Second World War Lorna Johnston worked as clerk typist at the Gasworks. 'If I remember rightly there were ten retort towers where the gas was made and the coke was the residue which could be sold out on the district. The coal trucks from the St Hilda Yard ran along the top and they tipped the coal into the retort house. One of my tasks was to calculate how much gas had been made in the previous 24 hours all over Tyneside at Howdon, Redheugh, Jarrow and South Shields and how much had been distributed to the factories which were all working 24 hours a day. We were very fortunate that we never had a direct hit on the gas holder, although we had a few near misses. We had to have security photographs taken so we could get in if there was an emergency. The photographer turned up and even the men whose faces were black from the retort house had their pictures taken. I don't know if the photographs would have been of much use.'

The gas works closed in 1957 when gas began to be piped in from Monkton Cokeworks.

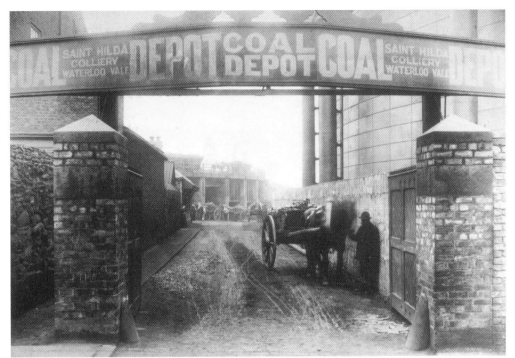

Waterloo Coal Depot, 1890. The gasworks stands to the right. A faint St Hilda Pitshaft can be seen in the centre of the picture. At this time the area in between Waterloo Vale and Station Road would have been the powerhouse of the town.

The Station Hotel at High Shields, 1891. Crossing Laygate is the St Hilda Waggonway. To the extreme right is a confectioner's shop. Outside is a horse tram.

An advert for A.J. Wares Ltd, King Street, *circa* 1909. Arthur Pegler recalls: 'The Theatre Royal in King Street had a company in residence called the Denval Players. They lived in the Roman Road area and were there so long that they became well-known in Shields. I can remember seeing Gracie Fields in the Empire Theatre next door in a production called 'Mr Tower of London' produced by her husband, Archie Pit.'

Jean Henderson and friend Mavis Gascoigne in King Street, 1957.

Inside the Town's Mosque at High Shields. From left to right are: Said Abdul Kaid, Mrs Hussein, Mr Hussein, Abrahim Hussein, Gamila Hussein, Mr Abdo Mohamed Kaid, Mrs Kaid, Mrs Zahra and Mr Nagus Zahra.

The Arab Community

Most South Shields people don't have to go far back in their family tree to find ancestors who were born outside of the UK. Arab sailors had been passing through South Shields since at least 1839 when Aden became a British Colony, but they only began to put down roots around the turn of the century when shipping patterns began to change. Wireless communication brought about the tramp steamer which according to telegraphed orders travelled from port to port, picking up and dropping off cargo instead of following long pre-arranged trade routs. Crews could find themselves discharged far from home. Tyne Dock exported more goods than it received. Steamers would travel in light from other British ports, pick up a cargo and then engage a full crew at the Mill Dam which made South Shields an excellent place for those seeking work.

Seamen waiting for a ship were required to stay in licensed lodging houses which tended to be run on nationality lines. The Masters of Arab boarding houses provided a variety of services to their lodgers: a line of communication to home for both money and letters, credit when needed and help with any difficulties with the local authorities. Holding a boarding house licence made a man a local institution and gave him a source of power. There are reports of Masters bribing ship's engineers to employ men from his house, and then the men would pay him part of their wages in return. One Master did so well that his business expanded to include a coach service to London.

Boarding houses did not always supply meals, encouraging the growth of Arab cafes selling traditional food and drink. While many stayed in Shields only until the next ship out, by the First World War many men were beginning to marry local girls and settle down. During the war labour shortages encouraged the government to classify many Arabs as British so they could serve on British Merchant Marine shipping whose own crews had joined the Royal Navy.

After the First World War the logistics of the coal trade did not return to normal. In common with most other pits the Harton Coal Company found its considerable pre-war exports to France, Italy, Spain and Germany were lost for good and production was now channelled into domestic needs which had lower demands for shipping. Tyne Dock coal exports, which had been as high as seven million tons in 1913, slumped to one and a half million in 1926.

Unemployment caused some local resentment with some forthright views being expressed in the *Shields Gazette* and many Arab seamen also became embroiled in inter-union disputes. However, by the end of the Second World War they were pretty much an accepted part of the local scene, and began to move out of the Mill Dam area and into the new housing estates of Cleadon Park and Harton.

Mr Kaid: 'I came to South Shields in 1956 because I had friends here with a lodging house and it was easy to find a job then. They helped me as much as they could. When you come to a new country where the language different and even the shape of the houses is different you can take time to become accustomed. But step by step you get used to it. My daughter was one of the bridesmaids when Muhammad Ali had his marriage blessed here. We were very proud. It was a big day for the Muslim community and for South Shields.'

Crowds out for the blessing of the wedding of boxer Muhammad Ali at the Mosque in 1977. Among the people at the front are: Ali Mobalh, Abdo Saif Abdula, Zafh Khan, Bill Lodge carrying a crown that was later presented to Muhammad Ali, Abdo Mohamed Kaid and Abdul Alli.

SECTION TWO

FROM THE BEACON TO THE BENTS

The Lawe Top … The Marine Parks … Westoe Colliery …
The Beach … Trow Rocks … The New Town Hall …

The Marine Parks seen from the ballast hills on the Bents, *circa* 1895. Although increasing numbers of visitors would be arriving via the new North Eastern Railway Station in Mile End Road, the area still has a very industrial look to it. Construction of the piers would not yet be complete and the Bents Park and the Promenade would still be in the future. Horse trams from Tyne Dock would make the Marine Parks accessible to the populations of Templetown and Corstorphine Town and even East Jarrow. Trow Quarry would be thriving and there would still be proposals to turn Trow Rocks into Trow Docks. The South Marine Park looks gaunt without its trees.

A group of soldiers stationed on the Lawe Top during the Second World War. The soldiers were barracked in corrugated iron huts at the top of Lawe Road, the site is now used as a children's playground. After the war, others found use for the barracks. Elizabeth Purvis remembers: 'As soon as they moved out the people we called the squatters moved in. Some of my friends were among them. They were some of the families who had been bombed out from Pearson Street and Fort Street. My dad helped them move in because they didn't have anywhere else to go. I remember going inside the huts and there was a big pot bellied stove in the middle and blankets hanging down from the ceiling to separate areas out for different families. They were there for some time. Then the council built them pre-fabricated houses and they moved out.'

Robert Wray then aged twenty months is on the right, with him is Beryl Jopling aged four years. They are sitting on the wall surrounding the old 'Gun Cannons' on the Lawe Top in September 1940. Behind them is one of the old brick faced navigation beacons that were once used to guide ships into the River Tyne. The terrace houses in the background were then occupied by the Chapman, Mountain, Gunn and Ford families.

The Harbour, *circa* 1910. The Groyne was constructed in 1884 as a wave trap to protect the newly dredged harbour. The light tower was erected by Trinity House and began working on 30th October 1887. One of the legs of the tower is hollow, allowing the weight that worked the foghorn to drop.

The *Adelfotis II* aground on the Groyne.

A wintry scene in 1958 with the Tyne Pilot Cutter *Guide* moored off South Shields Motor Boat Club. Jack Swinburn's Boat Building Yard is to the left. The Tyne Pilot Authority building is on the far right. Elizabeth Edmund recalls: 'Our family, the Purvis', have a long history of working as river pilots. Before

ship to shore radio the pilots had to go out and look for the ships. It was first come first served, and they were paid by the tonnage. Everyone would scramble for the big ships and some pilots wouldn't get a fair crack, so they decided to pool the money. Before radar they navigated through the river by depth soundings. My father had a big wooden table with the depths of the river on it. He would guide the apprentices through it with little wooden model ships.'

Left: The launching of the Wray family houseboat, *Good Intent* at South Shields Motor Boat Club in the early 1960s. On her first trip she was set on fire by vandals at Ryton and destroyed. She was converted from a ship's lifeboat by Harry Wray, a founder member of the club in 1946 and long time secretary. Centre front is his great friend, Joe Riggs, a River Tyne tugboat crewman.

Ocean Road County Secondary Boys School Class 3A in the school yard with teacher Mr Bob Whitfield in 1953. South Shields Marine School, now 'Kirkpatrick's Bar and Restaurant', is in the background. Included are; Colin Fairless, Derek Turbitt, Alan Bayes, Jimmy Hunter, Billy Robertshaw, Billy York, George Overton, Fred Lees, David Phillips, Noel White, Robert Wray and Alan McHugh.

The 1st South Shields Sea Scout Troop of the Congregational Church, Ocean Road. They are on stage in the Church Hall for a publicity photograph for the 1951 Gangshow 'Sea Fever'. The title is being spelt out in semaphore. Included are; Troop Leader George Smith, Desmond Hubb,  Ken Gibson, Billy Robertshaw, Jimmy Hunter, Allan Cullen, Gerry Booth, George Overton, Robert Wray and Stan Byers.

South Shields Station. The building was opened in 1879 by the North Eastern Railway to replace the much smaller Low Station near the Market in Station Road. The Stanhope and Tyne Railway had used the site since 1834 as workshops and a boarding point for

their passenger service towards Durham. Considering that the boundary of Shields was then at Westoe and the present Town Hall was over twenty-five years in the future, the building's extensive glass roof would have then had a size and magnificence rarely found outside of a church.

A *Shields Gazette* report of the opening tells how: 'Hundreds of sightseers who had no intention of making a journey strolled onto the platform to gratify their curiosity. On the previous night the 9.35 train from Newcastle was detained at the old station on its arrival there and was utilised for the conveyancing of the movable fittings to their new and more commodious resting place. Until the arrival at Shields of this train the telegraph lines connected with the passenger traffic could not be interfered with; and in this department men were promptly set to work with the satisfactory result that business could be proceeded with from the new building as early as required. The first to avail themselves of the new line of transit were the excursionists to Edinburgh and Glasgow at

4.55 am. To Sunderland during the day no less than 749 tickets were issued and to Newcastle 410. Altogether no less than 4,095 tickets were issued, or nearly four times the average for an ordinary Monday. The visitors to South Shields were chiefly from Sunderland.'

The last sections of the station building during demolition in 1998.

Mile End Road, looking towards the River Tyne, *circa* 1900. The area to the immediate left is now the multi-storey car park. The picture was probably taken from the tower of the Royal Assembly Rooms.

The Royal Assembly Rooms. They opened in February 1891 to cater for the richer members of the increasing numbers of visitors to the town. Decoration was by Mr Laidler of Newcastle. Air conditioning was fitted and there was a direct connection to the Royal Hotel. Some guests also stayed at the Golden Lion Hotel in King Street. Hotels such as this often had links with the stage coach industry. On 10th November 1882 a government inspector, Major General Hutchinson, was given lunch there after inspecting the council's new horse tramway on behalf of the Board of Trade. The inspection found several faults and the tramway was not able to open for business until August 1883.

The Marine Parks and Marine Parade, *circa* 1980. The Marine Park was officially opened on Wednesday 25th June 1890. Reclaiming the land for the North and South Marine Parks and the Bents Park involved the demolition of years of accumulated ships' ballast, and then landscaping the site and planting trees and shrubs. In 1854 alone 94,263 tons of ballast were discharged in South Shields. Reportedly, much of the ground under the South Park and the Bents is gravel from London which contained an array of exotic seeds whose flowers could still be found growing in the area until the 1950s. The parks represented a huge transformation of derelict land and a demonstration of what public finance and an elected town council could achieve.
They clearly impressed the 1890 edition of Reid's Guide:

'Entering the South Marine Park on our right, we can take pleasure in admiring the tastefully laid out walks and beds of flowers. A splendid promenade forms a conspicuous object at the centre of the Park, from which may be obtained a good view of the surrounding district. Model yacht sailing on the lake is a favourite pastime with many of the inhabitants, whilst wildfowl sport themselves on and around the little islands. The lake is well patronised by skaters during the winter months, the weather being favourable. Crossing over to the North Park there is a large Aviary containing several peacocks, blackbirds, owls and pigeons, with many other kinds of birds being added from time to time. A number of squirrels form an additional attraction. For those interested in games there is provision for Lawn Tennis, Bowls and Quoits, all the materials needed being provided at a very low charge.'

Two views of the South Marine Park. In the above view the park with its wide paved walkways and lake would still be a novelty to the townspeople. In winter the Corporation had the power to enclose the lake when it froze over and charge skaters for admission. *Below*: The bandstand has now arrived. In summer it would be a centre of social activity and in later years the surrounding tarmac would be sprinkled with chalk dust to assist dancing.

The South Marine Park, *circa* 1900.

On the day of the opening, at 2.30 pm, the official procession made its way from the Town Hall in the Market Place to the park by way of King Street, Fowler Street, Westoe Lane, Ogle Terrace, Wellington Terrace, Woodbine Street, Ocean Road and Seafield Terrace to the park entrance. The list of participants reproduced below gives a glimpse of the important social and economic groupings of the town at that time. It would also be interesting to know how the order of the parade was arrived at and if any jostling for position took place.

Police.
Band of the Wellesly Training Ship.
The South Shields Pilots.
The South Shields Volunteer Life Brigade.
The carriages containing Sir John R. Mowbray, Bart; MP; J.C. Stevenson, Esq MP; The Mayor, Canon Baily, Alderman and Councillors, The Town Clerk, and Corporation Officials.
Public Library Committee and the Lifeboat Memorial Committee.

West Docks Works Military Band.
Knights of Labour Society.
Railway Servants Society
Bricklayers Trade Society.
Ancient And United Orders Of Free Gardeners And Friendly Societies.
Band of the 3rd Durham Artillery Volunteers
Sailors and Firemens Union.
Ancient Order of Druids.
Royal Antediluvian Order of Buffaloes.
Oddfellows Friendly Society.
Amalgamated Society of Carpenters and Joiners.
Shipwrights Society.
The South Shields Borough Prize Band.
Boilermakers and Iron Shipbuilders Society.
Catholic Benefit Society.
Tailors Society.
Moulders Society.
Band of Green's Sailors Boys Home.
Members of Swimming Club.
Amalgamated Society of Engineers.
Smiths Trade Society.
Temperance Societies.
Ancient Order of Foresters Friendly Societies.
Band of Saint Bead's Chemical Co.
Police.

The Scooter Boats on the Marine Park Lake. Inside are; Ada, Joanie and Ellen Whitfield.

A group of children, 'Fishing for tiddlers' by the Marine Park Lake, *circa* 1955.

The Wouldhave and Greathead Memorial. Reid's 1890 guide describes the monument: 'On the side facing the approach from the town is a tablet bearing an inscription. Clocks, dog troughs and drinking fountains form a useful part of this very ornamental structure. On the west front is a very large medallion of Willie Wouldhave, surrounded by a laurel wreath with a model of the lifeboat beneath. On the north tablet, is a representation of the building of the lifeboat by Greathead, and on the south the saving of a shipwrecked crew. On the east is a tablet commemorating the Jubilee of Queen Victoria. The monument is 10 feet square at the base and about 45 feet high. The architect is Mr J.H. Morton of South Shields.'

Although the memorial is to Wouldhave and Greathead, their claims to be the fathers of the lifeboat are not undisputed. In his 1856 lecture Thomas Salmon made clear that there was more than one version of how the first purpose-built lifeboat came to be: 'The original lifeboat was built in South Shields by subscription under the inspection of Henry Heath, Michael Rockwood, Cuthbert Marshall, Thomas Masterman, Joseph William Roxby, and chairman Nicholas Fairles. The following is the history of the invention in the words of the chairman of the committee himself from a letter bearing the date the 4th February 1806, and it corresponds in every particular with that of my late father, who was himself an original trustee of the South Shields Lifeboat Fund, and well acquainted with the circumstances of the invention, I place the most implicit reliance on Mr Fairles' facts.'

Nicholas Fairles wrote: 'I do declare that neither Mr Greathead nor Mr Wouldhave was the inventor of the lifeboat. The truth stands thus. Several gentlemen formed themselves into a committee, of which I had the honour of being chairman for the purpose of obtaining information and models most proper for the purpose of saving persons from ships wrecked at the mouth of this harbour. Two models were produced; one of which was by Mr Wouldhave, which was not approved by the committee and Mr Wouldhave was presented with one Guinea as compensation for his trouble. The other, presented by Greathead, was also voted unsatisfactory, but he was not compensated as it was expected that once a decision had been reached on the lifeboat he would be paid to construct the vessel. Then Mr Michael Rockwood, an intelligent member of the committee, described a boat by which he was saved at Memal: she resembled the Norway yawl. The committee then endeavoured to combine with their own knowledge the information they had received and to produce out of the whole something which might answer the purpose. In one idea they all agreed, that the boat should be formed at each end alike; as described by Mr Rockwood; that the bottom should be something in form between the cobble and the yawl with breadth for two persons to row abreast and with proportional length; and with great elevation at the ends.

Some time later Mr Rockwell and myself by accident met and the conversation turned to the proposed boat. We entered an adjoining tile manufactory in East King Street and there endeavoured to explain to each other our ideas of the boat, by making a model in clay. In this we succeeded and the boat was built by Mr Greathead under the direction of the committee. Mr Greathead proposed that the keel should be curved and this is the whole that he has to any claim as the inventor.

Some years after I was not a little surprised at an application from Mr Greathead to sign a certificate, purporting that he was the sole inventor of the boat. My reply was that I could not consider Mr Greathead the inventor nor would I sign any certificate separate from the committee.'

According to Salmon the individual to whom Fairles was writing replied that the differences between Wouldhave's model and the boat as built were trivial. Fairles replied: 'The following points had been laid down by the committee as absolutely necessary in the formulation of the boat. Buoyancy, and the ability to divide the water with the least possible resistance. Each end of the boat was to be similar so as in leaving the wreck there might be no opportunity to turn the boat about. A great elevation at the ends was necessary to prevent agitated water entering the boat. Finally that the local situation required an easy draught of water.

Mr Greathead's model was of a long flat boat, nor were the ends alike. He described it as similar to a boat in which he had been accustomed to go up the rivers of America in the night time under the command of some navel officer. This model had no buoyancy, no cork, nor did it resemble the lifeboat. Salmon considered that too much time had elapsed for the matter to be definitively settled, but it was likely that no one individual has the sole honour of being the inventor of the lifeboat, although Greathead did build it and contributed one of its main elements, the curved keel. Mr Greathead was fortunate to receive several flattering compliments from persons of the highest rank, a diamond ring from the then Emperor of Russia, a Parliamentary grant of £1,200, 100 Guineas from Trinity House, 60 Guineas and then a silver medal from the Society of Arts and other gifts. Notwithstanding all this, he died a bankrupt.'

Interestingly Salmon does not comment on Wouldhave's claim to fame but simply describes him as: 'A housepainter and for many years clerk of St Hilda's Church. He died poor in this town on 28th September 1821, aged 70, and was distinguished during his lifetime for his eccentricity of manners, versatility of mind, and a peculiarly inventive genius. Honest as poor, and almost as communicative as ingenious he was always employed, yet always changing his employment; sometimes with shouts as if speaking with a deaf person, arguing on music with the organist and philosophising at other times with a keelman. He suggested an original improvement in the building of docks and amused himself by the construction of various curious instruments among which were an organ, a clock and an electrical machine. He was as original in appearance as manners.'

The Pier Pavilion building during refurbishment in the 1950s. The Pavilion has had a variety of players including Roy Doltrice, the Denville Players, the Gilbert and Sullivan Society, St Gregory's Players and the Westovians.

'The Boyfriend' at the Pier Pavilion. From left to right: Beryl Henderson, Jean Beck, Judy Elphinstone and Liz Ayre.

The Gilbert and Sullivan Society's production of 'The Student Prince' at the Pier Pavilion in 1965.

The cast of the 1964 Pier Pavilion Summer Pierrot Concert in the South Marine Park held during sports week. From left to right: Mary Proffit, Malcolm Boyle, Pauline Wheatley, John Murphy, Beatrice Mills (née Green), Joe Airey and Joan Markwick (née Baker).

The pier head after completion of the Lighthouse in 1895. The base of the pier extends another forty feet out. The 'Gardeners shed' beside the gates is a guard's van used to provide accommodation for men working on the pier. The construction of the North and South Piers were two of the greatest projects of the Tyne Improvement Commission. The establishment of the TIC in 1850 was the end of Newcastle Corporation's hold over the River Tyne and the beginning of a long series of river improvement projects. Newcastle's control dates back to at least the return of King Richard from the Holy Land and recorded complaints against it go back to at least the time of the Lord Protector Oliver Cromwell. Ralph Gardner of Churton on the north bank petitioned parliament over the Corporation's heavy handedness and aggression and asking that: 'The trust of the River Tyne be put into faithful commissioners' hands, the Mayor and Alderman of Newcastle having betrayed the trust reposed in them.' The duties on shipping that Newcastle collected were simply paid into the city's general funds. An enquiry later suggested that for every pound being spent on maintaining the river, two were spent on lighting, paving and cleaning the city streets. In 1813 Mr Rennie, a river engineer, pronounced that the navigability of the Tyne was deteriorating with the river becoming clogged with ship's ballast. He advised widening of the river in some parts, narrowing in others and the construction of a pier on the South side, all at a cost of £519,320. Little action was taken and the poor state of the river is given as one of the main reasons for the construction in 1834 of the Stanhope and Tyne Railway from Weardale to South Shields rather that the shorter route to Gateshead.

The Pier Works, *circa* 1900. The 1849 Tyne Conservancy Bill proposed to pass control of the river and its duties from Newcastle to a group of commissioners representing North and South Shields, Gateshead and Newcastle. As with any proposed relocation and reallocation of power and money, experts were brought to the Bill's public inquiry to defend one side's claims and rubbish the others, arousing vast amounts of public indignation, excitement and anger. The River Tyne Improvement Act became law on 15th July 1850. The river and its assets, dredgers and tolls and the like were handed over to the Tyne Improvement Commissioners who found themselves with debits of £100,000 and a yearly income of only £10,000.

Construction of the pier began on 15th June 1854 with the laying of the foundation stones. The Commissioners, Newcastle Corporation and the Brethren of Trinity House travelled by barge to the Market Place from where they joined a procession along German Street (Ocean Road) headed by local seamen and pilots to the Heard Sands. Two hundred men were employed on the works by 1859. Some of the immense problems are recorded in the diary of engineer John Oldroid: 'After dinner went down to the quarry, engine gone wrong and men off work but very windy, the sand blowing very heavy. On to the pier, the sea washing right over and the men tipping, wet to the skin. The sea is making breach into railway, went home and returned and found about two hundred yards washed away and longitudinal timber metals all to pieces.'

The next day he found: 'The railway in a complete ruin and wreck, a large quantity of the mass of the pier removed and washed down about the cranes which will have to be removed. The engine cannot get water.'

In 1862, Mr P.J. Messent took over as engineer. Divers fitted the foundations, often working in more than thirty feet of water. Around 200 wagon loads of stone arrived from Trow Quarry each day. The lighthouse was completed in 1895 – three years after the Groyne. By this time the harbour had been dredged and coal had been exported from Tyne Dock for over forty years. Mr Messent died a few days after around three hundred feet of the North Pier was breached in January 1897.

Members of the South Shields Volunteer Life Brigade with the Chronicle Cup at the Brigade House on the South Pier, 6th November 1948. The cup was won in the annual rescue drill competition with other North East brigades. The photograph includes: Captain J. Straker, R. Orr, C. Thompson, D. Tinning, A. Clavery, O. Nickson, A. Corrigan, H. Jack, J. Ferrier, W. Elliot, Harry Wray.

South Shields Volunteer Life Brigade stage a mock rescue near to the South Pier in the summer of 1948. Climbing into the breeches buoy is Harry Wray dressed as an olden day ship's captain with his bird cage. He was later the recipient of a Queen Elizabeth II, 30 year long service silver medal and served the brigade as Deputy Captain, Rocket Master and Historian. Shortly before his retirement in 1965, Harry and the brigade made a breeches buoy rescue for real when the *Adelfotis II* ran aground near the Groyne and the entire crew were safely brought ashore.

PLEASURE GARDENS ON THE FRONT, SOUTH SHIELDS

The figure of eight railway. Rumour had it that in the early days of the Second World War enemy agents had concealed themselves high up in its structure and sent signals out to ships at sea.

THE PROMENADE, SOUTH SHIELDS.

A general view of the promenade and fair looking towards the pier. The date is likely to be shortly after the end of the Second World War. Although the sand dunes are not yet higher than the promenade, the level is on the rise.

Inside one of the arcades on the South Foreshore. The re-opening of the fair in 1947 was one of the events that proved to the townspeople that the Second World War was really over. The arcade is now part of the Ocean Beach Pleasure Park. Within a few years the town's leisure industry would be booming and there would be talk of holiday camps being built on the Leas.

Michael Henderson on a rocket ride outside the same arcade in 1960.

A young girl on one of the rides during a Good Friday afternoon in the mid 1960s. A fairground Dalek lurks in the shadows.

Some of the guest artists appearing at the first Catherine Cookson Festival at the Bents Park. Included are; Bernie Winters, Bob Richie, Scarlet O'Hara, Allan Snell, Ward Allan and Roger the Dog. They performed a take off of 'Make Me Laugh' a popular TV show which Bernie Winters hosted and the others appeared on as guests.

Bill Reeve runs Beverly Artists who supplied the artists: 'Our bread and butter is supplying acts to workingmen's clubs and pubs from Redcar to Berwick and right out into West Durham. I also book what we call corporate events for local authorities like the Catherine Cookson Festival, hotels and cruise ships. We even produce our own pantomimes. Some of the very first artists we looked after were Paul Daniels and Cannon and Ball – when they were the Harper Brothers. Frank Carson started as a £10 a night pub comic around here. We had Englebert Humperdink when he was still Jerry Dorsey booked for a week in the La Strada and six workingmen's clubs. He had just released his first record as Englebert Humperdink and the week he was working for us his record went to number one.'

Right: A South Shields fire engine on display at the Bents Park. For many years the park has played host to many of the large municipal events; including the town's annual flower show.

A typical day on the beach in the 1930s. In 1925 a book of six tickets for bathing tents could be obtained for one shilling. The tents would be a source of consternation as well as revenue to the corporation with reports of unsanitary practices being carried out by some of the residents.

Frankie's cafe. For many years Harry Frankie ran his cafe on the South Foreshore. Underneath the tower was a counter that sold everything from ice cream to hot water and South Shields rock to buckets and spades. The brick built restaurant on the south end remained almost unchanged until he retired in the 1980s. Later the building was turned into a pub which rather unexpectedly caught fire in the middle of the night. The north end remained open a while longer then it too closed and the site was cleared. This picture was taken during the winter shortly after the fire, note the blistered paint on the tower and the gale swept sand that has covered the road and the forecourt. Standing in front are; Neil Tweddle and Julian Varley.

Westoe Colliery coal washer. The washer began working in 1954 using 550,000 gallons of water to wash 500 tons of coal per hour. Westoe, the fifth colliery of the Harton Coal Company, was sunk in May 1909. Originally called Benthouse, it was almost complete in 1916 although production did not begin until after the First World War One.

In 1957 the NCB announced almost £7 million of investments for the colliery and with the closure of Whitburn, Harton and Boldon by 1982 became the centre of the town's coal industry. At their maximum the coal faces were some nine miles away from the pitshaft.

A Skip Pocket under construction during the sinking of the 1,600 feet deep Crown Shaft at Westoe. Work began on the shaft in August 1959 and was completed by 1961.

The C. Motor and winding drum in the shaft at Westoe.

A Lee Norse Continuous Coal Miner on the surface at Westoe Colliery.

The Baguley Ltd built 1960 tower wagon stands outside of Westoe locomotive shed. In common with streetlight maintenance vehicles, the heavily insulated platform on top could be raised and lowered to allow work on the overhead wire system to take place. Under the Harton Coal Company emergency repairs were sometimes carried out on wires carrying up to 1,000 amps, although this was banned under the NCB. Nevertheless, engineers would always throw tools up to colleagues working on the platform rather than pass them from hand to hand.

A junction in the underground tunnels leading towards the coal face.

Jack and Elizabeth Smith who lived at the Bents Cottages.

Marrian Allen (née Squires) recalls:

When I was eleven I was diagnosed by the doctor as having 'nerves' as they used to call it. I was sent from our home in Byker to live with my Gran and Granddad, Jack and Elizabeth Smith at the Bents Cottages. The Cottages were old fashioned, even for those days, and had outside toilets with a long wooden seat with a midden in the back yard, that was emptied about once a week. If any young men were delivering coal to the coal house next door they would look in the trap doors to find who was on the toilet and to have a good laugh at them. Normally we would have to wash outside, but if we were poorly we could bring a bowl of water inside.

When I went messages for someone and they gave me money, I wouldn't dare tell Granddad or he would have the money from me. There was a shop down the road and the lady used to give me gobstoppers half price, because she knew where I lived, but that was only if the shop was empty.

Gran was deaf and there was many a time Granddad used to give her a slap because she couldn't hear something properly. She used to take me to the market to buy fruit and potatoes. The traders would have to shout and the children would make fun of her.

I used to go for a walk with the dogs along the sea front two or three times a day. After I came back from the tea time walk Granddad would send me to bed and then go off to the pub. If I wanted to go anywhere I had to climb out of the window, or Gran would let me out. I didn't like to let her let me out because she would get into trouble, so I would go down the drain pipe and to Mrs Gilpin's across the road. She was always good for a drink, or a piece of bread, or something like that and I would play with the children.

The day I had to go home, Gran took me to the bus station. She said something to me and had to shout and some children started to make fun of her. When I was on the bus they came back and pelted stones at her which I couldn't do anything about because the bus was pulling out. I cried all the way home.

The Footpath from Bents Farm looking south to Mowbray Road, *circa* 1900. Bents Farm was created by the outcome of a case before the Durham Court of Chancery in 1715 concerning a block of freehold land. The Bentley family were awarded an area of land that bounded the south side of Westoe Cemetery which became known as Bents Farm and the farmhouse as Bents House. Both were swept away by the expansion of Westoe Colliery.

Betty Heron's cottage. This was one of several cottages built at the Bents for the workers involved in the construction of the pier. It was later demolished around 1885 to make way for the development of the sea front.

The quarry offices at Trow Rocks.

Stone quarrying at Trow Rocks. In 1854 a gauge railway was laid through the sand dunes to Trow Rocks to transport stone to the pier and the Groyne. The excavations destroyed a local tourist attraction called 'The Fairies Kettle' – a stream of water inside a cave cascading down from one ledge to another into little hollows which looked as if they had been purpose built and then into a huge cauldron. Both quarry and railway kept operating as the parks appeared, the funfair grew up and Frankie's cafe began dispensing tea, hot water and ice cream to day-trippers and coach parties. In 1954 the TIC closed the quarry and railway and after a hundred years of operation the 'Beware of Trains'

signs were taken down from the promenade. In later years several pubs were built across the site of the railway, one ironically named, The Marsden Rattler.

Bomb damage at Hyde Street, October 1941. Lorna Johnston recalls: 'On the night of Thursday 2nd October 1941 I was with my friends at the Glebe Methodists Church when the sirens went. As there had been a bad raid two nights before, we all ran home. I went into the brick shelter in the back yard with my parents and the neighbours. In a few minutes there were bombers overhead and

then my life changed for ever. Our house took a direct hit. I was blown clear and into the next street, my parents were both killed. Part of the shelter came down on top of me and just my toes were sticking out. That was the only reason the rescuers were able to find me.'

The Town Hall. The date is likely to be shortly after the statue of Queen Victoria was removed in 1947. Arthur Pegler recalls: 'I can remember seeing the St Hilda Colliery band in brilliant red uniforms on the steps playing the test piece that had won them a trophy. My father had a furniture shop opposite the Town Hall. He died when I was fifteen and I was given permission to leave Westoe Secondary School early to keep the business going. In Victoria Terrace off Fowler Street was the Buttercup Dairy and I can distinctly remember the two girls who used to look after that. Next door was a florists shop called The Floral Depot run by a lovely couple called Mr and Mrs East. Strangely enough, opposite that was a garage run by a Mr and Mrs West. Opposite the garage was the building in

which we had the upholstery and cabinet making workshop. My father bought it for £1050. It was the last cheque he signed before he died.'

Two postcards of the Town Hall. *Above*: The statue of Queen Victoria is missing suggesting it was taken prior to May 1913. The image has been considerably retouched, note the buildings blocking Beach Road to the left. *Below*: Queen Victoria and the statues, 'The Town Hall Hussies', have arrived. They were paid for by a public subscription of £1,000 begun in 1901. 'Victoria' was the work of sculptor Albert Toft , described as, 'a gentleman from the South, every inch the artist with long flowing hair and bow tie.' In 1949 the statues were removed for road widening. A petition for Victoria to be re-sited at Cauldwell gathered over nine thousand signatures, but the statue ended up in a small public garden on the site of a builder's yard at Chichester. There she remained, gradually gathering pigeon droppings, until the Metro Station replaced the garden and she returned to the Town Hall, cleaned and polished and on a slightly damaged plinth.

The Mayoress of South Shields, Mrs John Wood 'At Home', November 1929. 'Mayoress at home days' made good use of the splendid interior of the Town Hall. The *Shields Gazette* described the occasion in 1929:

'The spacious and beautiful suit of rooms on the first floor of South Shields Town Hall were given extra touches of elegance and charm in the honour of the occasion of the 'At Home' which the Mayoress (Mrs J.W. Wood) held yesterday.

The Mayoress received her callers in the members' waiting room and the visitors passed through an avenue of overhanging palms, foliage plants and rich autumn flowers into the large committee rooms where tea was provided. The reception room was a luxury of floral and palm beauty produced by Mr Wm Thompson from his rarest specimens at the nurseries of the West Park. The Mayoress, her daughter and lady attendants stood in a gorgeous setting of stately palms, rich tinted croton plants and a profusion of ferns and flowers in season.

The large tea room was laid out with two islands of decorative plants, ferns and autumn blooms. From the centre of each island hung huge overhanging palms, including specimens of the Kintia, Phonex and Cocos reared themselves in stately beauty. The general effect of the scheme was heightened by a lavish display of delicate ferns, flowering plants and cut blooms prettily arranged on the window sills and accommodating niches of the building. Under a blaze of brilliant light the transformation was complete, and the ornate rooms of the hall have never looked more alluringly attractive.

Pleasing music was provided by the Misses Forsyth (piano and violin) who were accommodated in an alcove of palms and foliage plants arranged round the main entrance of the tea room.

The Mayoress wore a charming gown of gold Impreme Faconne with the new silhouette with increased length of skirt in two tiers, the ensemble being complete with black velour picture hat. She carried a lovely bouquet of scarlet carnations.'

Between the hours of three and five the *Gazette* notes there was a constant stream of callers including; Sir James Readhead Bart and Lady Readhead, the Lord Mayor and Lady Mayoress of Newcastle, J. Chuter Ede MP and Mrs Ede, the Mayor of Tynemouth, the Sheriff and Lady Sheriff of Newcastle, Colonel and Mrs R. Chapmen, Mrs John Readhead, the Mayor and Mayoress of Jarrow, the Mayor and Mayoress of Wallsend, the Town Clerk, Mrs Curburson, Ald, Chief Constable Wilkie and Mrs Wilkie, Mr and Mrs A.T. Flagg, M.S. Blair, Mr and Mrs A.J. Wares.'

The activities of the town's social and political elite were not always seen in such a favourable light. A popular local song, 'Always Ready, the lady and the chain' began with the rousing words:

> 'It was at the garden Party – you know the one I mean.
> Where all the Westoe gentry made a quite exclusive scene.
> Where the mounted Bobbies chased away the public from the gate.
> And the Mayor in his golden chain received us all in state.'

And then went on to describe how as the day of the garden party wore on and alcohol was consumed the Mayor, his friend 'Robert' and many of the female guests upheld the town's motto 'always ready' in a variety of situations. Exactly who the Mayor, 'Robert' and the guests were is speculation.

The Town Hall Council Chamber was not always as tranquil and on occasions debate in the chamber would become rowdy as the *Shields Gazette* would report.

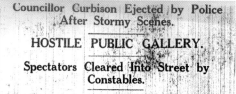

Councillor Curbison Ejected by Police After Stormy Scenes.

HOSTILE PUBLIC GALLERY.

Spectators Cleared Into Street by Constables.

For upwards of an hour the South Shields Council Chamber last night was made a veritable " bear garden " of dissension and uproar. A member held the floor during the whole of that time, refusing all appeals by the Mayor to resume his seat.

A resolution under the Standing Orders was passed to suspend the member (Coun. J. R. Curbison) for the remainder of the sitting, and finally a police constable was called in to eject him.

A violent struggle followed in which many of the Labour members combated the efforts of the constable to remove the councillor, the scene being one of a distressing character and lasting for several minutes.

Completely exhausted and beaten in the end, and with the upper parts of his clothing torn open and awry, the councillor was finally dragged out of his place and he no longer resisted the officer.

He left the Chamber violently protesting in words and with clenched fist. What he said could not be heard owing to the pandemonium which broke out in the public gallery.

Subsequently a number of policemen entered the back of the hall and at the request of the Mayor cleared the gallery, many of the occupants of which had secured their seats fully half an hour before the Council opened proceedings.

UPROAR AT COUNCIL

Violent Scenes During Discussion On Test Work Scheme.

SHIELDS LABOUR PROTESTS.

Member's Dramatic Dash Across The Chamber.

Disorderly scenes were witnessed at the monthly meeting of the South Shields Town Council last night, during a discussion on the question of test labour for men in receipt of outdoor relief.

Labour members took exception to a remark by Coun. J. W. Wood to the effect that they did not want the men to work, and when he accused Coun. J. W. Watson of having said that he did not want the men to work there was prolonged uproar.

Coun. Watson rushed across the Council Chamber, and, seizing Coun. Wood by the arm, angrily demanded a withdrawal of the remark. He was forcibly removed to a seat after an exciting tussle, but the disorder continued until Coun. Wood eventually withdrew the observation to which exception had been taken. Business was then resumed.

The Mayoress, Mrs Durey handing over a cheque for the establishment of beds at the Ingham Infirmary to Sir James Readhead Bart.

COUNCIL ELECTION,

MONDAY, 2nd NOVEMBER, 1925.

SHIELDS WARD.

The "LABOUR" Party, backed by COMMUNISTS and SOCIALISTS, is SCHEMING to CAPTURE the TOWN COUNCIL. IF IT SUCCEEDS the RATES will go SKY HIGH and your RENT WILL BE INCREASED ACCORDINGLY.

SOCIALISM in GATESHEAD has meant INCREASED SPENDING to the EXTENT of 12/6 in the £ on the RATES; equal to an INCREASED RENT of 2/3d. per week for WORKING-CLASS Tenants.

ELECTORS in GATESHEAD now know to their COST the VALUE of SOCIALIST PROMISES, and what VOTING "LABOUR" REALLY MEANS. DO NOT IMITATE THEM by "LOCKING THE STABLE DOOR AFTER THE HORSE IS STOLEN." LOCK IT NOW!

THE AIM of the "LABOUR" PARTY is NOT TO IMPROVE the ADMINISTRATION of TOWN AFFAIRS: but TO GRAB POWER in order to ESTABLISH SOCIALISM and COMMUNISM.

Wives and Mothers, the matter rests largely with you.

The "LABOUR" Party deludes the POOR and WORKLESS by CRACK-BRAINED schemes which have caused STARVATION and RUIN wherever they have been TRIED. An IMMEDIATE RESULT of the MAD "LABOUR" attempt to "SMASH CAPITALISM" will be:—

NO MONEY TO PAY POOR RELIEF, UNEMPLOYMENT DOLE,
OR OLD AGE PENSIONS.

The POLICY of the MODERATES is to ASSIST the POOR and WORKLESS until the AFTERMATH of WAR clears away; TO EASE THE LOAD OF RATES AS SOON AS POSSIBLE; and to GIVE LOCAL INDUSTRIES a chance to AGAIN CREATE PROSPERITY for SOUTH SHIELDS.

ENSURE CONTINUITY OF SANE LOCAL GOVERNMENT BY VOTING FOR—

R. FRED. HALL.

NOTE.—NEGLECT TO VOTE will simply MEAN PUTTING THE SOCIALIST NOOSE ROUND YOUR OWN NECK.

Printed and published by R. Simpson & Sons, Chapter Row, South Shields

---

MUNICIPAL ELECTION, NOVEMBER 1st, 1929.

Hadrian Ward.

To the Electors of Hadrian Ward.

LADIES AND GENTLEMEN,

At the request of a number of residents and endorsed by the South Shields Labour Party, I offer myself for election as Labour Candidate.

Unemployment is a serious burden upon the women and children and in their interests alone, steps should be taken to provide work. The Labour Government is offering increased Grants to local authorities and I will wholeheartedly support further schemes of work for the benefit of the town.

River Tyne Bridge. The development of heavy road transport demands that better facilities should be provided for crossing the river between North and South Shields. I am in favour of the erection of a bridge, believing that with a TRUNK ROAD through the borough increased trade and prosperity will be brought to the town.

Civic Welfare. South Shields is far behind most towns in the country in matters of health, housing and education. A Labour majority is needed on the Town Council to ensure ADEQUATE HEALTH SERVICES, SLUM CLEARANCE SCHEMES, ELECTRIFICATION OF STREET LIGHTING, AND FREE SECONDARY EDUCATION.

Poor Law. In April 1930 the Town Council will take over the duties of the Guardians, and it will be my endeavour to see that sympathetic treatment is given to those in need.

My experience of home management during the past ten years and acquaintance with the cares and responsibilities of the housewife in these trying times, leads me to especially solicit the support of the women.

Trusting to be honoured with your interest and vote on November 1st,

Yours sincerely,

Margaret Gallagher.

Two local election pamphlets from the 1920s. Note the appeals to newly emancipated women.

Westoe Lane, *circa* 1907. Other than the tram and the costumes very little in this image differs from today. The tram will shortly pass out of view to the right and stop at the car stop directly under Westoe Bridge.

The Glebe Girl Guides in 1947. We are now just a few hundred yards to the south, but today the view is very different. The bridge and embankment are now gone and the site taken by a car wash. The Glebe Church, which can be glimpsed to the left, is also gone, although the site remains empty.

CHICHESTER, LAYGATE AND WESTOE

Frederick Street ... The Palace Theatre ... Cuthbert Street ... Dean Road Depot ... Holdsworth's Cycles ...

Dean Road tram sheds probably just after the First World War. The third row of men are in military rather than Corporation uniform so they may be demobed ex-tram staff. The front row are point boys. The second row are management staff. To the right are a number of men in pill box style hats. They are likely to be inspectors. The main body of men are likely to be drivers and conductors. The men in the tramcar balconies are the depot painters and handymen. Amongst their duties would be painting the advertisements on the trams. A number of men are sitting on wooden boards slung between the balconies. The trams themselves were originally delivered as open top cars. The Corporation later rebuilt them with covered tops although both upper and lower decks remained open at the ends for many years.

South Frederick Street. The workmen replacing the blocks in the road and the lack of passengers on the tram suggest that this is before the service opened in 1906. The man in inspector's uniform in front of the tram may be Austin Huntly. The shop later became Hugh Robson's cake shop. Dennis Boad recalls: 'The line in Frederick Street was made of thick wooden blocks with the tram lines set into them and every few years oil was sprayed on to them to stop them rotting. When they took up the lines, the blocks came up as well and at night everybody was taking them to burn. They were so soaked in tar they lasted for ages.'

The Palace Theatre. Dennis Boad recalls: 'My father was a member of South Shields Glider Club and they use to have exhibitions of model planes in the big Foyer at the Palace. Some were driven by elastic bands and others by petrol motors.'

An advertisement for A. Turnbull, Watchmaker and Jeweller.

Children of Laygate Lane Methodist Chapel, 1951. Margaret Henderson is in the back row, on the right.

Cuthbert Street, *circa*, 1910. The Old Durham Billiard Hall was located on the left. The town abattoir was at the end of the road and escaped animals would often be seen running around there. Butchers' boys would have gone there for general offal. For the more refined meats, such as ox-tail and tongue, they would have visited Swifts near the end of the street. A Mosque was located at the top of the street near the Lord Clyde public house.

Laygate Lane, *circa* 1910. The Tivoli Theatre is on the left. Lawrenson the butchers would be on the next block up. Further up is Turnbull's the clock shop, then Daker's the butchers. It is reported that the chief constable once asked for the cancellation of the Tivoli's dramatic licence on the grounds that the holder was sentenced to nine months at the Durham Assizes for offences under the Bankruptcy Act.

Hanlon's Store, Eldon Street, 1933. Outside are; Elizabeth Horseman, Mary Jackson, Ada Simpson and Olive Hopper

In the back yard of 71 Frederick Street *circa* 1930. At the back are: Winifred Hancock and Betty Dawes. In front are: Patricia and Dennis Boad whose father worked as a Corporation tram conductor.

Below: An outing from the Unionist Club in Frederick Street, outside Freeman Hardy and Willis in 1950. Included are; local singer Harry Hartley who is holding a banjo, Dickie James and Sammy Leader.

Horse tram staff, *circa* 1900, probably at the Victoria Road Depot. Privately operated horse trams began in the town on 1st August 1883, the company going bankrupt in April 1886. This is likely to be the second company which took over on 28th March 1887. The angle of the tram body to the track suggests it is a 'reversible' model which allowed the body to be swung around at the terminal without unhitching the horses.

A South Shields horse tram dumped in a field. This may well be shortly after 1st February 1906 when the privately owned system closed down to allow the Corporation to begin construction of their electric tramways. As the depot was in Victoria Road the location could be in the Westoe/ Chichester area. The 'passengers' may have been out for a Sunday stroll when they found this abandoned tram body and used it as a prop for an unusual family photograph.

A Corporation electric tram in pristine condition outside the Dean Road Depot. The advertisements on the side suggest this may be after the system opened for traffic in June 1906. The buildings at the back are stables and a wholesalers' store house from which a Mr Thompson sold salt. The system began life with twenty similar  cars, soon increasing to thirty-five. Over the years the Corporation constantly upgraded and enclosed its stock although car No 7, often seen pictured as the first official car to reach Tyne Dock, survived in its original condition as a stores car until it was broken up in 1938. On 8th April 1938 Mayoress Nancy Bradley set fire to a tramcar in the forecourt of the depot to mark the arrival of the trolleybuses.

Corporation buses in Dean Road yard. Dennis Boad recalls: 'I started working on the trolleybuses in 1949 on what we called boys' money, £7 a week. When I turned twenty-one I went on to full pay, £9 a week. My father Fred Boad died in Chichester Depot on Boxing Day  1955. He had complained of feeling unwell, went upstairs to the club for a quick drink and suddenly collapsed and by the time he got to hospital he was dead. He started working on the trams in 1929 at £2 10s. It wasn't big money but it was regular, although men didn't get paid until they were actually on duty. If you were in the drivers' room the inspector could send you outside to clean the tram windows but that didn't count and you wouldn't get paid for it. Even when I used to travel on my dad's tram to give him his tea 'can' I used to have to have a ticket. The conductors became so used to running up and down the tram stairs that they hardly used to touch them. They just swung themselves around on the rail. I used to walk around the house with my dad's bus conductors pouch on. It shined with age.'

Dean Road, *circa* 1928. This area is currently occupied by shops belonging to Blades Barbers and the Children's Society. The house pictured here later became Sayer's fruit shop. John Stanley Parker is at the upstairs window, the identity of the woman outside is unknown.

Below: Norman and Marion Fay who run Holdsworth's cycle shop in Dean Road with some of their collection of vintage cycles, including a model built in 1917 by a Mr Guthrie who made cycles and model train sets and ran a shop in Cuthbert Street.

SECTION FOUR

HARTON TO MARSDEN

*Cauldwell ... Harton Village ... The Vigilant Inn ... The Grange
And The Hall ... Harton Colliery ... Around Marsden ...*

Harton Village, *circa* 1890. The village possibly predates South Shields itself, 'hart' apparently derives from the old English word for 'hill of stags' and 'ton' from the word 'stronghold'. The ivy covered building on the right is the Ship Inn which dates back to at least 1804. Harton Lodge would be directly behind the Ship, the white building towards the centre is the old Vigilant Inn and behind it is the roof of Harton Grange. Across Sunderland Road is Harton Hall and St Peter's Church built from stone quarried at Cleadon Hills. Harton was incorporated into South Shields by Act of Parliament in 1921 against the wishes of the village council and many local people. Feelings apparently ran so high that locals torched the village records rather than hand them over to South Shields Council.

CAULDWELL, HARTON, SOUTH SHIELDS

A 1930s postcard of the junction of King George Road and Sunderland Road. Minute examination reveals that the houses on the left of Sunderland Road are still under construction. Construction began on King George Road dual carriageway in July 1921. One hundred and twenty feet wide with a tramway down the middle, the route would appear very impressive to the inhabitants in the cramped streets around the riverside. Municipal disagreements prevented the road and the tramway from directly reaching Sunderland and King George Road never became the artery into the town it could have been.

The high standards of the Corporation's highways and parks and Gardens Department are evident in this 1950s view of Cauldwell roundabout.

Marsden Road under construction in 1931. The camera is probably outside what is now 49 Marsden Road.

Cuthbert Nicholson on air raid patrol in Harton House Road.

Cuthbert Nicholson and his daughter, Judith, residents of Marsden Road.

Moor Lane East looking towards the Vigilant Inn, 1920. South Farm would be on the left. The camera appears to be located opposite what is now 41 Moor Lane East.

St Mary's Avenue. The bungalows on the right are built on the site of the old duck pond and may predate the construction of Marsden Road. The farm on the left is now the site of a series of bungalows constructed by Ridley the builder. Ridley Grove is named after him.

Above and left: Weddings at St Peter's Church. Although now very much enclosed by housing St Peter's still retains much of its former rural atmosphere making the church a very popular place for weddings. The French Gothic style church was built in 1867 on the site of the 1836 Harton Oratory at a cost of £1,650. The church accommodates around 200 worshipers. In 1993 the Rt Rev David Jenkins, Bishop of Durham dedicated the new north wing.

Harton Lodge. This building stood on what is now the grassed area at the junction off Marsden Road and Sunderland Road.

Below: The junction of Moor Lane and Sunderland Road, *circa* 1880. St Peter's Churchyard is just out of the picture to the right. One of the buildings visible down Moor Lane is dated from 1878 and now forms part of the Jet Garage.

The Vigilant Inn on Sunderland Road. Harton Lodge is visible between the trees. Robert Wray recalls: 'The Vigilant public house occupies the site of what was once Harton Turnpike Road and Common Cart Road. The present building dates from 1925 and was erected on the site of its demolished predecessor of the same name. The first building consisted of a small bar with cellar and five rooms plus three cottages containing six rooms and a stable, yet its exact origins are unclear.'

The old Vigilant could date back to at least 1833 although the name may have then been the Two Horse Shoes. The earliest record of the name of the Vigilant Inn was in 1872, so why would a country pub three miles from the Tyne change to a nautical name? Part of the answer is that shipbuilder John Readhead's owned an interest in the pub, his name appears on an 1866 management deed. However, the sign above the main entrance depicts the one funnel wooden tugboat *Vigilant* built by Readhead's two years later in 1874. However, three similar tugs are also registered in Shields under the name *Vigilant* in 1848, 1849 and 1860. So it is possible the 1874 tug is named after the pub which for some reason was named after an earlier tug.

The back of Harton Hall, 1893. The front of the building is very familiar on Sunderland Road as Posh Wosh and the Reptile House. The gardens stretched as far down Moor Lane as the church school. The camera is looking towards Moor Lane and the pond is in the middle of what is now Moor Avenue.

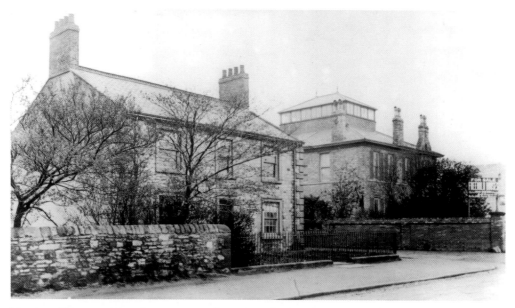

Harton Grange. The Grange stood on Sunderland Road where the Village Police Station now stands. Later The Grange was demolished and a line of terraced houses built along Sunderland Road to the garden of Wyngarth House. Later still, this part of Grange Avenue was itself demolished to provide a site for the Police Station. Following a gas explosion under one of the houses in 1966, Harton Residents' Association was formed. The site of the building on the right is now the forecourt of Harton Garage. A map dated 1916 shows the building gone and a tennis court between the road and Moor Lane East.

Right: Joseph and Ann Jane Wray, the great-grandparents of Robert Wray, outside the front door of their home at 19 Double Row, West Harton, *circa* 1914. Born at Newbrough near Hexham in 1842, Joseph came to Shields with his brother James to work at Harton Colliery in the 1860s. He eventually became a Master Shifter, a senior official in charge of coal filling shifts, and directly subordinate to the Colliery Overman. He was the recipient of an Illuminated Address in recognition of his fifty years service with the Harton Coal Company.

An inspection party at Harton Colliery on 21st August 1895. Among the party are: Mrs C.W. Anderson, Doctor Murphy from Sunderland, Mrs Marshall Stephenson, Mr and Mrs O'Callaghan from London and Mr A.L. Langman. Work was officially started on the Colliery in 1841 and was complete by 1844. Its 1,200 ft shaft was one of the deepest in the area.

Harton Colliery, *circa* 1910. The pithead area has been very much rebuilt. The HCC was replacing steam with electrical power and its pits were some of the most advanced in Europe. During the Second World War the pit was a likely target for German bombers. In August 1940 a formation of around thirty Heinkel 111s appeared over the town and Bob Jewitt who was working at the colliery as a time office lad had the responsibility of warning the workers to take shelter when enemy planes were expected. Bob recalls taking shelter near the railway bridge over Harton Lane but to his surprise the bombers passed peacefully over the town like a military parade.

A group of workmen pictured shortly before the outbreak of the First World War at the Cleadon Park residence of James Kirkley, the agent and majority shareholder of the Harton Coal Company. Centre front is Joseph Wray, joiner, carpenter and cabinet maker and grandfather of Robert Wray. He lived in Harton Village at Willis Cottages, and was the husband of Catherine Stephenson, whose family managed the old Vigilant Inn.

A tramcar speeds along the light railway between the lanes of King George Road. The location is possibly approaching the roundabout on the west end of the Nook with the row of houses behind being Central Avenue. The tramcar No 39 is rebuilt from a 1914 model and carried the name of the Tyne pilot cutter *Protector* whose crew were killed when the ship was sunk by enemy action in December 1916. The name was painted out in 1934.

A trolleybus lies on its side after an accident on Marsden Lane. Barry Dobson recalls: 'I think the driver was pulling away from the Marsden Inn, over the bank top to come down towards Fulwell Avenue. At Hampshire Way there was a big trench across the road and the buses would often jump when they went over it. It was this particular driver's first day, and he might have hit that hump, but whatever happened the  bus crashed into one of the traction poles that held up the wire and fell on its side. As it turned over the conductor jumped off the back and fortunately the driver got out with just a scratch on his nose. The bus itself was a write off.'

An aerial shot of the area around Redwell School. One of the first tasks South Shields Corporation set itself in 1850 was the clearance of the town's appalling slums. This process took well until after the Second World War. And echoes of the old problems can be found in tenants' manuals of the 1960s. 'The tenant shall not shake mats or carpets over the railings of the house or out of the windows, or break firewood in the house or on the stairs or passageways … The tenant shall immediately report to the medical officer any cases of infectious diseases in the house … The tenant shall not drive nails into the walls of the house.'

Tents were often used as semi-permanent accommodation on Marsden beach as well as the North and South Foreshores. Here a group of young people pose for a photograph while enjoying a weekend at Marsden.

Sam Gilpin, car park attendant at the Marsden Grotto in 1957. Sam was seventy-seven and lived in the Bents Cottages. He worked at the Grotto for five years.

SECTION FIVE

TYNE DOCK

Readhead's ... Coal, Warehouses And Cranes ... The River Postman ... Slake Terrace ... The Deans ...

Teaming Coal at Tyne Dock. As the coal cascade down through funnels or chutes from the wagons on the staithes above, men would be required to smooth it out across the hold of the barges. The dangers and filth associated with the job are obvious.

An early picture of Readhead's Yard at the West Dock.

Readhead's, 19th July 1927. The official party at the launch of SS *Sir David* built for the Gas Light and Coke Co. of London. One of shipbuilding's most famous names, John Readhead began his business in a yard in Pilot Street in 1865. Readhead started the yard in partnership with John Softly. Both had previously worked for Marshall's of Willington Quay, Readhead as engineering manager, Softly as general manager. They dissolved their partnership in 1872 with Readhead continuing the business in Pilot Street. By 1881 the business had outgrown the yard and Readhead now in partnership with his sons bought the West Docks and began to relocate the business there. Still playing a very active part in the business, John Readhead died on 9th March 1894, two years before the move was complete. Under his son James, Readhead's became a private limited company in 1909, at the same time as a serious slump took place in the shipping industry. The company kept investing in new machinery and a new dry dock was completed in 1913. Sir James Readhead died in 1930 and was succeeded by his son James Harold Readhead. During the depression James fought hard to bring orders into the town and was well regarded by his workforce. Those who remember his era speak of a great family feel to the yard. James died unexpectedly in 1940 as the yard was grappling with the demands of the Second World War. After the war, the yard was rebuilt and a large area of land in Corstorphine Town was taken over in 1945.

A general view of construction work underway at Readhead's Yard.

"Happy be the issue of this good day."

★ ★ ★

Opening Ceremonies.

THIRD DAY:

THURSDAY, FEBRUARY 4TH, 1909.

CHILDREN'S DAY.

The Bazaar will be opened at 2·30
in the afternoon by

Miss Muriel Readhead.

Chairman:

MASTER SCOTT PAGE.

A Company of Young Children numbering
about 30 will assist at this Ceremony.

Opening Hymn:—"All things bright and beautiful."
Opening Prayer:—Master George Firth.
Votes of thanks by Children
SONGS BY CHILDREN
"At our Bazaar."
"When Grandmamma was Young."
"Story Land."

Miss MURIEL READHEAD.

Muriel Readhead, one of the shipbuilding family, pictured in the official programme of Chapter Row Wesleyan Centenary Bazaar, 1909.

Bomb damage to the Yard's joiners and sawmill shops caused on the night of 9th October 1941.

Some of the workforce at Readhead's Yard pose for a publicity photograph after a successful ship launch in 1975.

Bob Plum the River Postman, the location may be near Readhead's Cut. Bob started in the Post Office in 1882 at 19s a week. His round consisted of delivering letters to ships moored on a three mile stretch of the south side of the Tyne from the river mouth to Jarrow Quay. The Pill Box type hat he is wearing suggests this may be before the First World War. After forty-two years service with the Post Office, thirty-five on the river, he retired in 1934.

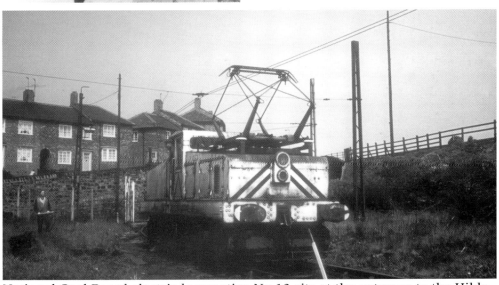

National Coal Board electric locomotive No 13 sits at the entrance to the Hilda Hole Sidings, *circa* 1975. Behind it is Portberry Way. John Temple's 1810 waggonway would have run from his Templetown Pit up to where the locomotive is standing then sharp left to run under Commercial Road to the Templetown coal drops. To the left is the 1835 Brandling Junction line which at that time carried the British Rail service to Newcastle. Today both railways have gone and Portberry Way looks down on a combination of leafy footpaths and industrial developments.

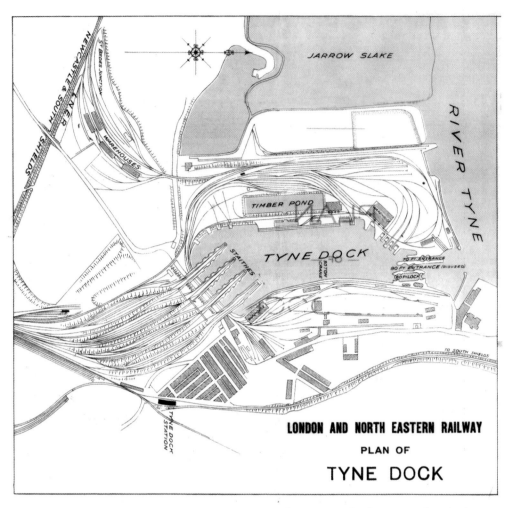

A London and North Eastern Railway Plan of Tyne Dock showing the timber ponds, the four massive coal staithes and the twenty-five miles of sidings that channelled in coal from the Durham coalfields. Unlike the Albert Edward Dock on the North bank, Tyne Dock was built by the North Eastern Railway Company rather than the Tyne Improvement Commission. Earlier plans for a dock in the area had been drawn up by colliery owner Simon Temple in 1803. After several other aborted schemes the first pile was driven on 3rd March 1856. The Chairman of the North Eastern Railway let water through the sluices into the dock on 26th December 1858 accompanied by the sound of cannon fire. At its maximum the pool covered 50 acres. By the mid 1920s there were four massive timber gravity-operated staithes fitted with forty-two spouts and electric belts and conveyers that could ship coal at around 450 tons per hour. In 1930 there were fifty-five cranes running off electric, hydraulic or steam power, fifteen warehouses and thirty graving docks. In 1937 the TIC took over the dock from the LNER for £800,000. In 1954 an Iron Ore Terminal was completed on the west side and by 1956 the plant was discharging 1,360 tons of imported ore each year. At one point the dock was handling the entire ore traffic for the Consett Steel Works.

The entrance to Tyne Dock, looking towards the River Tyne. On the right a ship can be seen under construction in Readhead's Yard.

Tyne Dock Pool. This view conveys something of the level and variety of trade using the dock.

One of the large warehouses at Tyne Dock Pool surrounded by cranes.

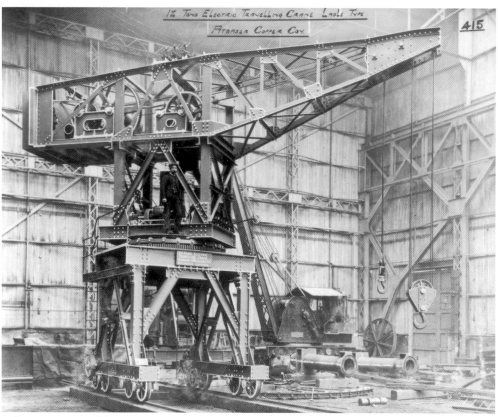

A lever arm grabbing crane, 1950.

The railway lines running across Tyne Dock arches to the staithes. Tyne Dock arches were built to carry the coal traffic that poured into the town from the Durham coalfield over the main Shields to Jarrow Road.

Tyne Dock arches seen from the road level. As coal traffic dwindled the wooden coal staithes were gradually run down and dismantled – by 1967 they were closed completely. However, the 'slime dripping arches' themselves lingered on as a reminder of the town's coal trade until they were demolished in 1977.

SLAKE TERRACE, TYNE DOCK.

A postcard showing Slake Terrace at Tyne Dock. Included amongst the shops is a Norwegian cafe and the North Eastern Hotel. This was a lay over point for the four tramcar routes on the town's figure of eight shaped system. The line connecting with the Jarrow and District Electric Traction Company's route can be glimpsed to the left. The relationship between the two systems was rarely happy. Although the horse trams before them also reached Tyne Dock they came via Templetown while the electric trams by-passed the area and came through the surrounding houses of Frederick Street.

While they lay over their tramcar at Tyne Dock conductor Frederick Boad and driver Jimmy Edwardson pose for a photo taken by a travelling photographer in 1931.

Almost thirty years later a trolleybus pulls into Slake Terrace on the same route as the tramcar on the opposite page. By this time Slake Terrace had been demolished to allow larger cargoes in and out of Tyne Dock. Since then most of the buildings to the left have also gone and many of the streets that were vitalised by the arrival of the electric tramcar in 1906 have either been swept away or become quiet backwaters.

At the top of Stanhope Road a trolleybus turns towards Tyne Dock. Passengers, particularly those heading up Boldon Lane regularly used the opportunity of the bus slowing down for the roundabout to jump off .

Killen Cottage at the Deans, *circa* 1906. The embankment behind carried the 1834 Stanhope and Tyne Railway, the first passenger railway to reach Shields. Today it carries the Metro.

Below: Flooding around the Deans Brewery at the end of Dean Road in 1900. The brewery was pulled down in 1920. Over the years South Shields has been well provided with drinking places. In 1834 there were around 150 inns or taverns and five common breweries. This area has always been vulnerable to flooding which may explain why the triangle of land in between the HCC and LNER railways was not developed for housing until 1932, long after Harton was absorbed into the borough to increase the supply of building land.

The Fruit Shop at Corstorphine Town. The shop belonged to Joseph Kennedy and Ellen Kennedy (right).

Tenants of the Deans Estate, *circa* 1951: Ada Whitfield, Sally Lunn and Ellen and Joanie Whitfield.

Sisters Joanie and Ellen Whitfield standing outside 11 Thames Lane on the Deans Estate in 1954. They are dressed for Mass to be taken at the St Peter and Paul's Roman Catholic Church at Tyne Dock.

A group of Catholic children who were pupils at non Catholic schools being given a meal at the parochial house of St Peter and Paul's Roman Catholic Church in Tyne Dock. They would have just had first communion.

A party of women on the platform at Tyne Dock Station in 1920. Included are; Edie Wilson, Francis Dixon, Mary Blacklock, Elizabeth Gibson, Ada Whitfield, Ellen Kennedy and Louisa Seddon. The Deans Estate is in the background.

SECTION SIX

PRIVATE JOY AND PUBLIC CELEBRATION

Peace Day ... Church And Social ... Sporting Moments ... Musical Interludes ... In The Sky And On The Air ... The Long Awaited Day Dawns ...

Good Friday at the Market Square, 1925. Mr W. Owen, who had not missed a Good Friday gathering for seventy years, is being congratulated by the Mayor for his attendance record. Although this is the Roaring Twenties, Mr Owen's style of dress harks back well into the previous century and shows how elements of one era can linger well beyond the next.

Ocean Road, very probably during the town's celebration of Queen Victoria's Diamond Jubilee in 1897. Ocean Road would then be known as German Street and the North Sea the German Ocean. The offices of the South Shields Scottish Association stand next to the Marine School. The building on the left may be the offices of the South Shields Gas Company. The Jubilee came at a time when the town council was showing increasing confidence in itself. It marked the event with concerts in the North Park, Market Place and West End Park, the decoration of the Market Place, King Street and Ocean Road with banners and flags, an organised meal for two thousand of the town's poor children and six hundred poor old people, bonfires on the Beacon and ballast hills at South Park and staged firework displays in the North and West End Parks.

The baker John Henderson announced they would present to the parents of every child born on 22nd June an iced ornamented birthday cake if a valid birth certificate could be produced, and the town allowed the inmates of the Workhouse outside from 2pm until 8pm.

A group of Shields children in patriotic costume. Their identity is unknown although the photograph carries the names Helen, Betty, Bea, Bea, Dorothy and Me.

South Shields Members of the Northumberland Hussars pictured in 1914. Back row: Cpl Purvis, Pte Robson, Sgt J. Scott, Pte A. Parlett, Pte W. Welsh. Front Row: Pte F. Towning, Cpl Gentles, Sgt J. Gilroy, Pte J. Tweddle.

Below: An advert for a First World War patriotic picture screened at the Palace.

How Britain Prepared for the Big Push

PΛLΛCE, High Shields.

ALL NEXT WEEK
Twice Nightly - AT 6.50 and 9

BRITAIN PREPARED

Under the patronage of The Mayor (Alderman Taylor), and Mayoress and Members of the Town Council of South Shields,

PEOPLE OF SHIELDS can satisfy-themselves how

BRITAIN HAS PREPARED
FOR THE GREAT WAR.

There are SEVEN REASONS why everyone should witness this Gigantic Spectacle.

1. Because 'BRITAIN PREPARED' is the only authentic pictorial presentation directly sanctioned BY HM Government.

2. Because there will be nothing shown in Shields and District during next week to approach the splendour of this PICTURE, and probably never will be again.

3. Because 'BRITAIN PREPARED' depicts the work of the Navy and Army as no other production is allowed to show.

4. Because you will see the GRAND FLEET IN THE NORTH SEA; the fleet which recently proved how effectively, 'BRITAIN PREPARED'.

5. Because 'BRITAIN PREPARED' enables you, as it were, to march with the troops from the Drill Ground at Home to the Trenches and Battlefields Abroad.

6. Because no greater tributes could be paid to the memory of the late LORD KITCHENER than a full appreciation of his great work which made 'BRITAIN PREPARED'.

7. Because it is the duty of every Britisher, young and old, to satisfy themselves how.

BRITAIN HAS PREPARED.

The Children's Peace Day Procession heading down Mowbray Road on its way to the South Marine Park. The camera would be on the bridge which carried the Marsden Rattler. Bents Cottages would be to the right.

The end of the First World War was marked with Peace Day on 19th June 1919. The *Shields Gazette* commented: 'The Town Hall, the Queen Victoria statue, the Wouldhave Memorial and Lifeboat, the public shelter, pier parade and other prominent public places have been richly adorned with festoons and streamers of fluttering flags, shields and electric devices. Many of the principle buildings in private ownership have carried out huge schemes of decoration, the main thoroughfare being a blaze of fascinating colours. There is an irresistible infection about the display of the Union Jack. Someone makes a beginning and a flag is hoisted out of a window or lashed to a gate post, and hey presto! in a few hours the whole street or avenue is transformed into a sea of patriotic colour and animation.

During the day the St Hilda Colliery band played a work called 'Victory and Thanksgiving' in the South Marine Park. In the North Marine Park the Harton Colliery band performed 'The Hymn of Peace' and excepts from Faust. Dancing took place on Sea Road to music provided by the South Shields Concertina Band.

The Mayor and Mayoress (Coun and Mrs T. Sykes) could not have had a busier time. They were here there and everywhere. They were at the children's demonstration in the morning, they attended the entertainments to the crippled children and the blind in the afternoon, received the salute and march past of the Victory Procession at the Bents, and after his Worship had addressed the huge crowd there assembled, and made a few presentations, he and the Mayoress passed on to the choral concerts in the South Marine Park. In addition to all these engagements the Mayor read the Royal Proclamation at seven or eight different places.'

'God Save The King' is sung at the Bents. On the stage are the Mayor, Coun Thos Sykes and Lt-Col Robert Chapman DSO CMG.

A First World War tank is formally accepted by the Town Council and fixed in position at the Lawe Top on 18th June 1919.

A Victory Tea is served to a large group of children in Waterloo Vale. The lady seated in the big arm chair is likely to be the Mayoress, Mrs Sykes. Two rather expensively dressed children can be seen at the bottom right, while many of the children will be from St Hilda's Infants School. A long arc of bystanders appear to be watching the children eat.

Below: A Victory Tea is served in the Corbridge Street area. The identity of the participants is unknown. Apart from one very young boy all of the participants are women.

Agnes Woodcock aged sixteen in 1926. The photograph was taken at Speedo Photographs behind the Picture House in Ocean Road

A portrait of miner, Tom Smith.

Evelyn Lawrenson aged seven.

Helen and Joan Whitfield at Helen's First Holy Communion at St Peter and Paul's Church.

Pupils of Mortimer Road School.

A cookery class at Baring Street School, *circa* 1950. Every girl would make their own cookery outfit by hand the year before the cookery classes commenced. Sarah Smith (née Barry) is third from the left in the second from front row.

Mr and Mrs Otto Carlson with their eldest son John. Otto was born in Gothenberg. He was at sea during two world wars being torpedoed in the first and serving in supply ships during the second.

From left to right: Elizabeth Wilkinson (mother of Albert and Joyce) with her brother Tom and sisters Florence, Dora and Sally, 1917.

Shields evacuees Valerie and Rita McGinley pictured while in the South of England.

Postman Dennis Boad relaxing after his round. He worked for the GPO until his retirement in 1994 and now collects GPO memorabilia.

Bill Lodge at twenty-two years of age when he served on the *Black Toft*. The ship was sunk on 22nd February 1945 by Captain Oppendorf who also torpedoed the *Kelly* off the Tyne.

Bill Lodge with Captain Richard Annand who was born in Westoe Village and was the nephew of Lady Barbara Chapman. He was the first person to be presented with the Victoria Cross in the First World War.

Bill Reeve and his wife Edith with their son Bill in 1939.

Ready to go to war. Trevor Tate with Catherine and Margaret Freeman in Egerton Road, 1940.

Christmas at the Missions to Seamen, 1952. Dorothea Shell recalls: 'Christmas at the Seaman's Mission lasted for forty days. We use to start in November and keep going until the end of January so everybody arriving over the period could take part. On Christmas Day itself we would have two hundred sailors in the dance hall, all nationalities, and they were all given a present. There would be activities every night, a concert on a Monday, dance on a Tuesday, a film on a Wednesday, a dance on a Thursday, Friday was free, a dance again on a Saturday and church on Sunday. Around 1950 Pardre Smith started the Hostesses Guild and appointed a committee who vetted the girls before they were allowed to become hostesses. They all came either from the town's churches, Marks and Spencer's, Binns, or were nurses. We kept going until 1984 when we closed and reopened as the Cellar Club.'

Two photographs of pupils of Laygate Methodist Chapel preparing for their
Christmas show in 1952.

Children of St Bede's Central School, 1928.

Pupils of Gilbert Daniel's School of Dancing at Westoe Village in 1945.

Ellen Kennedy in front of a Studbaker Car belonging to Amy Rogers, *circa* 1954. Amy ran the gown shop opposite the Town Hall in which Ellen worked.

Left: The Gilpin Family who lived at the Bents Cottages in 1932. At the back are Kaye, Leslie and Jimmy. Leslie worked at Morgan's the bakers in Lord Street and later bought Gowdie's curtain shop in Jarrow. At the front are daughter Emma, father Sam, mother Edith and son George. George worked at the Coal Washery at Westoe Colliery and later as a bus conductor.

Marchers from the town's churches of many denominations taking part in the Good Friday service at the Market Place in 1947.

Robert Wray and his mother Mrs Hilda Wray outside their home at 102 Greens Place, the Lawe Top on Good Friday 1953. That morning they had attended the annual march and the religious service at the Market. Robert was a member of the South Shields Town Mission Band and was wearing his uniform, in colours of navy blue with red piping and gold epaulettes, for the first time.

The Glebe Church Carnival of 1927.

Glebe men in a mock wedding, *circa* 1932. The bridal party includes; Ged Parkin, Arthur Siddel, Roy Parkin, Lance Best jnr and Harry Wright

The Glebe Queen and Retinue pose for a photograph.

The Glebe Church's production of 'Babes in the Wood', 1952.

Members of South Shields Gliding Club at the West Park.

The Glider Club, *circa* 1929. The glider has the name 'Renault' on the tail. Bob Renault was the founder of the club and was killed in the Second World War.

Members of the South Shields Branch of the Radio Society of Great Britain celebrating the return of transmitters after the Second World War. Dennis Boad recalls: 'John Read, the Borough Engineer was a keen amateur radio enthusiast, he and my father used to talk about wavelengths all the time. Sometimes they would play 'seventy-eight' records over the air. When the war started the police came and took their radios away. During the war they asked my dad to help track down a signal which they thought was coming from South Shields to Denmark. One member, a Scotsman Harry Forester, could talk fluent Norwegian and became a spy in Norway. He never came back and we assumed he was shot.'

Society Members in the West Park. John Tyzack is in the back row, John Reid second from right and Walter Dennal is second from the left.

Stanhope Road School Football Team, 1912-13. On the left in the middle row is Billy Walker who served in the First World War at the age of sixteen. He later worked at Harton Colliery and was a member of the Home Guard in the Second World War.

South Shields Association Football Club, 1919-20. This was the club's inaugural season in the Football League. The photograph was taken at Horsley Hill in August 1919. Elected to the League by virtue of an outstanding record in the North Eastern League before the First World War, the club experienced only moderate success in the following eleven seasons and moved to Gateshead in 1930.

Dean Road School Team, 1948-49 season. Included are: Benny Billens, Billy Dent, John Young, Ridley Alan, John Lascells, George Post, Eric Grey, Norman Brampton, Stidolph and Les Carpenter.

South Shields Boy's Club presentation night at the Hedworth Hall. Included are: George Post, Rolly Smith, Joe Dickinson, George Defty and Billy Howie.

A group of Shields footballers in the 1950s. Included are: Chris Young, John Walker, George Post, Jimmy Rea, Sid Brown, George Curry, John Collins, George Byers, Harry Kircald, Arther Turbett, Les Newsome and Jimmy Allan.

Marsden Colliery Cricket Club visiting South Hetton in 1960. Members included are: Organiser Matty Smith, John Carlson, Harry Eden, Davie Seagrove, Albert Dunn, Mr Dawson, Mr Brown, Mr Berry and Alan Stokoe.

A table tennis knock-out competition in 1958. YMCA 'B' beat the Tyne Dock Youth Club. Included in the picture are; Ian Carlson, Bob Coverdale, Hugh Slater, Billy Henderson and Bob Newham.

A football match at Harton Recreation Ground. Harton Colliery is in the background, Geordie Atkinson is among the players.

Charles Crookson's New Hawaiian Swingtette at the Hedworth Hall. The band performed between 1946-53 and here featured; Bob Osbourn on Hawaiian guitar, Charles Crookson, vibes, Dougie Lumbsdon on drums, Wilfe Wood on bass, Ethel Hindshaw, vocals, Sid Parkinson on accordion and Ken Goodall on piano. Ken Goodall remembers: 'The band was formed just after the war and began playing in the Miners' Hall at Bede Street for a pound a night. Sometimes when we were playing at receptions the lights would go off and someone would have to find a shilling for the meter. One of our television appearances was on the Tyne Tees Talent Show from the Majestic Ballroom.'

The Ken Goodall Trio performing on Tyne Tees Television's 'Golden Disc Talent Finals' in 1960. The group won first place in the instrumental section. Among the judges were, film star Jack Payne, Anne Heywood, TTTV director George Black and Programme Controller Bill Lyon-Shaw.

The Ronnie Callahgan Octet, winners of the 1952 Danceband contest at the Majestic Ballroom. Included are: Bill Chapman (bass), Ronnie Callahgan (piano), Eric Gamblin (guitar), Stan New (drums), Art Mowat (alto), Bobby Car (trumpet), Eric Pollard (tenor) and Alan Mitchell (trombone). Eric Pollard began playing the saxophone aged fourteen in 1944 with Eddie Mordues Band at the Queens Hall. He recalls, 'I was playing a solo at the Hedworth Hall when this guy came up with a beer in his hand and poured it inside my saxophone, drunks like him think it goes up the sax, but it doesn't, it just lies there. I finished my solo and he was still standing so I poured the beer back over his head to a round of applause from the band.'

Left: Eric Pollard in 1946.

Christmas Eve at the Majestic Ballroom in 1955 with Billy Henderson and Jean Slater.

Below: The staff Christmas party at the canteen in Newman's lingerie factory in 1955. Included are; Jean Slater, Mavis Davidson, Eva Meeks, Margaret Meeks, Ann Wright and Dorothy Lowery.

The Boys' Section of Tyne Dock Youth Club, 1953. Included are: John Stobbs, Ken Todd, Gordon Watson, Stan Hutchinson, Tommy Duffy, Norman Saleh, Ron Davison, Dave Johnson, Peter Bengstein, Bill Henderson, Paul Watson, Les Thompson, Keith Inkster and Alan Bengstein. The occasion was the purchase of a guide dog by the club after collecting one ton of silver paper.

Tyne Dock Youth Club Girls' Section, 1953. Included are: Alice Benson, Doris Johnstone, Margaret Eskdale, Kathy and Margaret Watkinson, Silvia Raine, Joyce Blacklock, Brenda Green, Jean Wright, Ann Peel, Silvia Capling, Lilian Johnson, Moira Pollard, Mirabelle Mills, Shirley Bengstein, Olive Watkinson, Chris Young, Dorothy Whittington, Chris Tikis, Shirley Addison, Mrs Whales, Mr and Mrs McArther, Gloria Wiloughby and Jenny Pollard.

The wedding of Dennis Slater and Esther Carr in 1953 at St Cuthbert's Church in King George Road. Also included are: best man Arthur Slater and far right bridesmaid Jean Henderson, aged fourteen.

The wedding of Irene Smith aged nineteen to Harold Wilson at Harton Methodist Church in 1960. Irene is seen here with her father, Tom Smith.

William Hardy and Elizabeth Hardy on the occasion of their Golden Wedding Anniversary held in their home at 36 Taylor Street. William worked for many years as a crane driver at Tyne Dock.

Joe Tindale, Kathleen and Cuthbert Nicolson and Madge Hunter with other members of their family in their back garden on Harton Lane in 1932.

Beatrice Glover outside her home on Harton Lane in 1936.

Bill and Rosalind Reeve in South Eldon Street, 1949.

Albert Wilkinson, Joyce Carlson (née Wilkinson) and their uncle Tommy Smith in the backyard of 20 Alma Street. Tommy worked at Harton Colliery most of his life.

Barry Dobson at St Joseph's JMI School in Fellgate with a South Shields Corporation single deck bus. The bus is preserved and has spent many years at the Dean Road Depot. Barry took the bus to the school to demonstrate how public transport has changed in South Shields.

Photograph Acknowledgements

Shields Gazette
Pages 2, 7, 15t, 19t, 23t, 34, 41, 45t, 45b, 50t, 53t, 83t, 119t, 119b.

South Tyneside Libraries
Pages 9, 10b, 11b, 17, 19b, 31, 57t, 57b, 58t, 58b, 59t, 66t, 66b, 73, 74b, 75t, 76t, 76b, 78t, 78b, 79t, 79b, 80t, 87t, 87b, 88t, 93t, 93b, 97t, 97b, 99, 101, 183, 185t, 186b, 187t, 188b.

Newcastle City Library
91t.

Beamish The North Of England Open Air Museum
Pages 18t, 20, 21, 22, 23b, 24t, 26, 27t, 27b, 33, 38, 53b, 54b, 55b, 55b, 68t, 68b, 70b, 71t, 81b, 83b, 92b.

Robert F. Mack
Pages 4, 12t, 12b, 13.